Home
52 Ways Back to

ELAINE PATTERSON

Other Books by Elaine

Reflect to Create! The Dance of Reflection for Creative Leadership, Professional Practice and Supervision with accompanying Workbook and Reflective Journal

Our Humanity@Work Working with the 7Cs – the 7 Human Capacities – for Insight, Learning and Change: A New Lens for Coaching, Coaching Supervision and Executive Reflection Reflective Journal and Workbook

With Jackie Arnold

Tomorrow's Global Leaders Today: Executive Reflection: Working Wisely in Turbulent Times

With Karyn Prentice, Anne Berthelin, Agathe Potel, Jean-Francois Thiriet and Pascale Venara

Superviser de Couer à Couer: Guide pour les Superviseurs, Coachs et Accompagnants

Elaine has also written numerous chapters, articles, workbooks and blog posts. Links to these can be found on her website.

For the seeker in all of us.

Homecomings: 52 Ways Back to Ourselves

Copyright © 2024 Elaine Patterson

All rights reserved. No part of this publication may be reproduced, distributed, or transmitted in any form or by any means, including photocopying, recording, or other electronic or mechanical methods, without the prior written permission of the publisher, except in the case of brief quotations embodied in critical reviews and certain other noncommercial uses permitted by copyright law.

ISBN: 978-1-9164560-1-3 (Paperback)

ISBN: 978-1-9164560-3-7 (eBook)

First printing edition 2024.

'Home is within me and always was.'

Richard Wagamese

The Most Important Thing

I am making a home inside myself.

A shelter of kindness where everything
is forgiven, everything allowed – a quiet patch
of sunlight to stretch out without hurry,
where all that has been banished
and buried is welcomed, spoken, listened to – released.

A fiercely friendly place I can claim as my very own.

I am throwing arms open
to the whole of myself—especially the fearful,
fault-finding, falling apart, unfinished parts, knowing
every seed and weed, every drop
of rain, has made the soil richer.

I will light a candle, pour a hot cup of tea, gather
around the warmth of my own blazing fire. I will howl
if I want to, knowing this flame can burn through
any perceived problem, any prescribed perfectionism,
any lying limitation, every heavy thing.

I am making a home inside myself
where grace blooms in grand and glorious
abundance, a shelter of kindness that grows
all the truest things.

I whisper hallelujah to the friendly
sky. Watch now as I burst into blossom.

A poem by Julia Fehrenbacher, reprinted with her kind permission

Contents

Foreword	xii
Introduction	xiv
The Soliloquys	1
Route Mapping	3
Stilling	4
Sanctuary	8
Slow	11
Silence	15
Solitude	18
Start	21
Safety	25
Senses	28
Soul	31
Self	34
Soul Friends	37
States of Being	40
Sacred	43
Salute	46

Footprints 49
  Seasons 50
  Savour 53
  'Seeing' Another 56
  Soften 59
  Sadness 62
  Surrender 65
  Shadow 68
  Suffering 71
  Stagnation 74
  Shape 77
  Stories 80
  Shame 84
  Sublime 87
  Seeking 90
  Serendipity 93
  Scanning 96
  Symbols – and Sideways Thinking 99
  Surprise 102
  Simplicity 105
  Silliness 108
  Souvenir 111

Rest and Return   115
  Strolling   116
  Spirit as Love in Action   118
  Skills for Life   121
  Study   124
  Stitching   127
  Structure   130
  Strength as Courage   133
  Service   136
  Society   139
  Stewardship   142
  Sharing   145
  Sorry   148
  Support   151
  Sleep   154
  Self-Care   157
  Solace   160
  So   163

Author's Note   167
Acknowledgements   169
End Notes   171
Bibliography and Reading List   187

Stepping Forth

Foreword by Karyn Prentice

In this beautifully presented book, the reader is met with an exciting opportunity, via years' worth of weekly invitations, to discover more about their personal homeland and inner landscape. It is a book to come back to again and again. Belonging is not a one-time event: it colours and flavours our choices, preferences, and perspectives. Some invitations will beckon us to leave the well-known for new territory, while others will remind us of treasures, we already possess but have temporarily lost sight of along the way.

What is true is that all of Elaine's soliloquys are rare and tender moments of life's holy music to help us locate the soul's one true note, that is ours and ours alone. Her book is a lighthouse illuminating the path to home.

Songlines are both a navigational aid and a repository of cultural knowledge for the aborigines. This book helps the reader put together what is needed, what is sensed but perhaps forgotten, and what is longing to be known by us if we but take the time, still ourselves, and create both a sanctuary and an awareness of what is singing us into existence – guiding our path as we read, write, and wander. Here, we are invited to gently listen for the music that resonates for us, that will tempt us down into our selves for deep reflection.

Within the journaling practices there are opportunities to embrace each word, engage with our own material and process, and be amazed at how far we have come. Then, with a pause, we can travel onwards. As Elaine suggests, you can pick up this book at any page and start from any word that draws you.

Each soliloquy is like a golden thread layering into the next, each note into the adjacent one weaving a tapestry of homecoming, belonging and love. Drawing upon Elaine's naturally abundant resources and inspiration they offer you a chance to claim and reclaim new and refreshed insights into who you are and your infinite capacity to be in and of the world.

Carry this book with you! Greet it like an old, beloved friend that you know you can trust. Set out on this journey – and on your wanderings you will find priceless pearls.

From Stilling to Solitude and from Self to Soul this book is a bow to the art of imagination, to deep reflection, and to the radiance of finding the lights of home on, the kettle whistling and warm music saying, 'Welcome Back'.

Introduction

Dear Reader,

Welcome to *Homecomings*: 52 Ways Back to Ourselves – a collection of reflective soliloquys. It is my hope that with it, we can each explore what it means to belong and how to come home to ourselves as a regular practice. I feel that the invitation to find our ways back home should be the foundational heart-based practice for our times. It has never been more necessary or important if we are to live with joy, beauty, generosity, compassion, courage, kindness, wonder, reciprocity, wisdom and grace.

My process of free writing found me listing vital words for living that began with the letter S. It was fascinating how trusting my apparently arbitrary approach has led to this body of work, which includes what emerged as the most important soliloquys to me.

Finding our way back to ourselves can be as frustrating and elusive as it is enriching – as we try to catch the threads of wisdom that life is trying to show us. It is a continual process of feeling lost and found, of arrival and departure, of disconnecting and re-connecting and of forgetting and remembering. The destination is always moving and can never feel complete because we are already changed in our setting off. As we learn to hold these frontiers for ourselves, our understanding of life and living deepens with each encounter.

This is not a fast book but one to feast on. The 52 reflective soliloquys invite you to reclaim old ground, discover new horizons within yourself or get back on track. Please note that they are not intended to be comprehensive but are to be used as invitational prompts for your own reflections. Each soliloquy is accompanied by a Songline – with both a creative and a reflective journaling practice – which can be used to take your curiosity further if that feels right for you. In Australian aboriginal culture, the term 'Songline' is used to describe a song that is sung to help people find their way.

Start where you are. You may choose to work through the book in the order as set out in the Contents or you might prefer to just dive in with whatever title grabs your attention. Either way, I hope this will become your own self-care kit which feels relevant and contemporary for you each time you open it.

Sending you love

Namaste!

Elaine

The Soliloquys

'We are all visitors to this time, this place.

We are just passing through.

Our purpose here is to observe, to learn, to grow, to love … and then we return home.'

Australian Aboriginal Proverb

Route Mapping

'The desire to go home….. that is a desire to be whole, to know where you are, to be the point of intersection of all the lines drawn through all the stars, to be the constellation-maker and the centre of the world, that centre called love. To awaken from sleep, to rest from awakening, to tame the animal, to let the soul go wild, to shelter in darkness and blaze with light, to cease to speak and be perfectly understood.'

Rebecca Solnit

1. Stilling
2. Sanctuary
3. Slow
4. Silence
5. Solitude
6. Start
7. Safety
8. Senses
9. Soul
10. Self
11. Soul Friends
12. States of Being
13. Sacred
14. Salute

Stilling

'Look at a tree, a flower or a plant. Let your awareness rest upon it. How still they are, how deeply rooted in Being. Allow nature to teach you stillness.'

Eckhart Tolle[1]

When we are still, life arrives unbidden.

To still is to stop and let life come to us. In our stilling we can start to pay exquisite attention to what is arising within us, as we also notice the beauty and resilience of nature around us.

Stillness – like our breath – is already here. It is not to be sought but to be remembered. Stillness is the antidote to a spinning self and a spinning world. Stillness – when we settle and ground ourselves – connects us to ourselves and to the rhythms of nature. In our stillness we can dive into our own depths as we commune with life.

Stillness is not to be confused with absence or emptiness. Stillness is full of presence and dynamism. To paraphrase Lao Tzu 'to the mind that is still the whole world surrenders'[2]. Stillness speaks. In our stilling we learn to listen with open ears to the music of life and the universe. We can give ourselves permission to catch up with ourselves. We can appreciate the wider current and webs of connection and interrelatedness with all things. We can hear our soul talking. We can glimpse the mysterious and the eternal. We can catch hints of what is wanting to emerge – the green shoots of the future – which are already present but we have been too busy to notice them. We can become our own compassionate witness, coming to appreciate that we are not our thoughts and feelings. These arrive like clouds in a summer sky and then float away.

Having a 'stilling spot' – a favourite place where we can contemplate, be it a favourite armchair, tree, a walk or a corner of the patio – is hugely comforting and resourcing. To paraphrase Jon Kabat Zinn, these are places where we literally have nothing to do, nowhere to go and nowhere to hide[3].

The Quakers have a long-established practice which they call 'Sitting in Silent Waiting' or 'expectant waiting'. For the Quakers, this 'centring down' is a time to become inwardly still in order to create an opportunity to experience God or the Spirit.

Learn to perceive yourself as the still point of the turning world[4]. If we carefully watch any of the great actors, musicians, artists, writers, performers, and leaders we will notice how they move only when they have first connected to the radiant still point within themselves. This still point is the pivot and the ballast for what follows. In this stillness and from the still point we can all connect to our sources of inspiration, intuition, integrity and intention.

Homecomings

As Lao Tzu provokingly asks us[5]:

> Do you have the patience to wait
> Till your mud settles and the water is clear?
> Can you remain unmoving
> Till the right action arises by itself?

Songlines

An Embodied Practice: Finding your Stilling Spot

Find your Stilling Spot. Your Sit Spot can be anywhere special to you. It can be in your garden, in a field, in a park, by a river, up a mountain or by the sea. You may choose to have more than one. But the key is to ritualize your Stilling Spot by committing to sit there for about 15 minutes (or more) at around the same time of day every day for a week (or longer). Still yourself through a grounding exercise and just be. Allow the weather and the natural world to come to you. Allow yourself to become alive to the hues, smells and textures of life around you. Tune into what is wanting to emerge within you. Journal or sketch what you notice when you still yourself.

Or, like the Quakers, you might like to try sitting with another in silence. Agree to sit in silence together for, say, 5 minutes and set your timer. Sit opposite each other and gently rest your eyes, not initially meeting each other's gaze until much later on in the practice. Just be with each other and gently notice what is happening in you, and between you. When the alarm goes off you might want to reflect on your experience of being together.

A Journaling Practice

In your journaling practice explore your relationship with stillness – is it friend or foe or something in-between? When you are still, what feels different in your body? When stillness speaks how do you listen? How can you find your still point in a world of action?

Sanctuary

'Sanctuary is a dose of grace.'

Terry Hersey[1]

Our sanctuaries are our very own oases of bliss.

A sanctuary is our own special sacred place – which we have created and holds energy and meaning for us. It is where we can push the pause button and return to ourselves. A sanctuary is a hearth in the heart centre of our life, where we can warm ourselves from the cold blasts of life's ups and downs. Joseph Campbell, author of *The Power of Myth*, called it our 'bliss station'[2] – a beautiful place of rest, ease and grace.

A sanctuary can be anything we make it or want it to be – a room, a ritual, a journal, a practice, a friend, a place in nature or a place we hold within ourselves – but crucially, it is just ours and ours alone. The very acts of naming and designating it are intentional acts of promise and commitment to ourselves. Having our own sanctuary (or sanctuaries) is also actually a deliciously radical act of defiance and self-care. The very process of intentionally building our own special sacred places – where we can gift ourselves an even deeper and richer experience of life – feels both intoxicatingly subversive and necessary. It is both a statement and a declaration of self-love to find a different way of being in a world which is always noisy and always busy.

We go to our sanctuaries for calm and to restore ourselves: to let the worries of the day dissolve; to listen to our warm hearts; to commune with our wild souls; and to hear the voice of grace. Our sanctuary is our safe place where we can retreat, muse, dare to dream and make sense of life. William Blake called it a time and place in each day where 'Satan could not find us'[3] – a spacious space where we are free from everyday obligations and pressures to experience our experience, to remember who we are and find our inspiration.

Our sanctuaries are places where we can always find a loving welcome – where we can be by ourselves to find ourselves and remember who we are as life seems to tug us in the opposite direction, sapping our attention and endlessly demanding this or that. Our sanctuary is a special place which we know we can return to again and again when we need a refuge, a virtual hug, a temple or a different well to drink from.

Songlines

Invitation: A Room or Space of My Own

Design and create your own spaces. These can also be in nature. Empty it or fill it with the books, pictures, flowers, plants, crystals, candles, quotes, music, objects, and furnishings you love. Make your own altar. Create your own rituals like burning incense, lighting a candle, or meditating as you enter and invite your space to open you up to touching and receiving grace.

Homecomings

A Journaling Practice

What sanctuaries do you need and want to create? How could you re-purpose what you already have?

'Nature does not hurry, yet everything is accomplished.'

Lao Tzu[1]

Our imaginations need time to meander, to wander, to wonder.

Going slowly is a deliberate choice to go mindfully and gently through the day. It involves paying focused and exquisite attention, to staying present and to intentionally relating to experience as it unfurls and unfolds before us in the now before it is gone.

But 'going slow' or 'going slower' is very hard to do. Despite what is now understood about the wellbeing and creative benefits of going slower, many of us still find great difficulty in slowing down in practice. This cognitive dissonance – the distance between what we know and what we actually do – compounds our feelings of failure. Speed is still expected and prized in many organizations. Efficiency is exalted over effectiveness. Social media torturing us with multiple feeds which frays our attention and plays into our fear of missing out, The constant multitasking and switching between our different roles and personas – made more acute

by the trend towards homeworking – forces us into hypervigilance as our minds struggle to contain it all. Self-imposed pressures and expectations trap us into 'doing more' or 'being more' in an endless cycle of diminishing returns. The scale of what must be done to contribute to our current humanitarian and environmental crisis creates new levels of anxiety.

And rushing from A to B, like a high-speed, out-of-control train can make life feel bland and tasteless. We forget to count the cost of our speed. We remove ourselves from the deep connection we need with ourselves, for nature and to life to flourish. We can forget to notice the beauty that is all around us. We override our evolutionary programming which was not made for an industrialized world. We can fall out of synch with the natural rhythm of our own breath and heartbeat, the natural rhythm of our own journey through life, and the natural rhythms of Mother Nature which – if we allow it – can both hold us and guide us.

Our bodies need rest. They need us to modulate our speed so we can catch up with ourselves. Even when we are busy, we can bring moments of 'slow' into whatever we are doing. Going slow (or slower) frees us to pay more minute attention to whatever we encounter as we travel[2].

Going slow helps us to calm our parasympathetic nervous system – which is always in super alert and hypervigilant mode, perpetually scanning our environment for real or perceived threats – supporting us to come back home into relational presence with ourselves and with others. This could be as simple as remembering to breathe or pausing to look out of the window. Our imaginations need us to meander, wander, marvel and wonder, so that we can feed our creative souls. Going slow enables us to create pauses (both micro pauses and longer pauses) in our crowded schedules. Only then can we choose between our routine reaction and a more creative response.

Our intention – and how we show up in the world – is shaped by where we choose to rest our gaze and what we choose to pay attention to. Going slower in this way enables us to lay down new neural pathways which can bring us back home to connection and to our humanity. The urgent need for us to go 'sloooow' helps us to creatively find our own balance, our own ground and our own spaciousness. Can we – or dare we – slow down faster?

Songlines

Invitation: Pause Points

Throughout your day, set reminders on your alarm clock to invite you to slow down – to breathe deeply, to journal or to look around you to admire the beauty of a flower on your desk or the view from your window. Look up at the clouds. Light a candle. Choose a bud or a leaf on a tree and observe its changes every day. Imagine you have a speed dial inside you, notice when you are exceeding your own set speed limit and take steps to slow down.

Homecomings

A Journaling Practice

What is your relationship with speed? How easy is it for you to 'go slow' or to 'go slower' – and where could you start? How might going 'slower' be hard for you?

Silence

'To see how nature – trees, flowers, grass – grows in silence, see the stars, the moon and the sun, how they move in silence … and we need silence to be able to touch our souls.'

Mother Theresa[1]

In silence, the music of life reveals itself.

Often, we find ourselves – and others – rushing to fill silences. Silence can make us feel uncomfortable. But the sound of silence enables us to tune into the essentials of life – to our breath, to our hearts beating, to the birds singing and to nature's universal harmonies. Silence returns us to the source of life when we can remember who we are and why we are here. Silence is needed if we are to hear our wild souls speak. In silence we can find an eloquence and a music, listening for the questions which are our own notes and harmonies, but which we may not hear in the cacophony of our daily lives. In our silence we might also be able to hear the whisperings from our ancestors as well as the murmurings of what the future is asking of us in the present.

Silence frees us to develop a deeper intimacy and a richer communion with the essence and source of life. In our silence we are reminded of our inter-connectedness and inter-relatedness to the world. The silence of another or other worlds beckons us. Here we are learning to listen from the spacious wholeness of our animal body and from a place of generous hospitality and courage. Perhaps we are even willing to be changed by our listening.

The sound of silence is needed if we are to hear the 'Om' of life – the spoken essence of the universe. Om is a sacred sound, syllable or mantra in Hinduism and is said to be the essence of the supreme Absolute or pure consciousness. It arises from the eternal silence of the universe and is the ultimate reality – one of Atman or divine feminine energy. Atman is a Sanskrit word that means inner or true self, spirit, or soul, beyond the identification phenomena or personality.

This communion can be like a prayer – that we have to return to again and again to hear the sense of the golden threads of our uniqueness and our belonging – our 'note' – as it calls us home. This 'responding' may also be thought of as a type of pilgrimage. Our strategic mind may be oblivious to this as it wants to return to the superficial safety of its checklists – distrusting the innate wisdom of our wild souls and warm hearts.

Perhaps the most important gift we can offer another both for ourselves and for others is a truly attentive listening silence.

Songlines

Invitation: The Sound of Silence

Create opportunities for you to hear silence. Listen for the silences between speech or activity. Sit in a wood, or a field or by the shore and listen to nature's symphony. Listen to the noise of the weather around you. Listen to the sound of your own body breathing and moving – perhaps even feel your heart expand. Sit in silence with another and feel the relational connection between you expand and grow.

A Journaling Practice

Try this. Switch off all your devices. Ground and centre yourself. Allow yourself to be held by your surroundings as you tune into the sounds around you. Tune into background noises, name them in turn and then let them go. Now bring your attention to the quietness within you. Now place your hands on your gut for 4 to 5 minutes and ask it what it wants you to know. Listen in the silence. Then place your hands on your heart for 4 to 5 minutes and ask it what it wants you to know. Listen in the silence. And then reach your hands out to represent connection with your spirit or soul or God and ask what your soul wants you to know. Listen in silence. And finally, place your hands on your head for 4 to 5 minutes and ask your head what it wants you to know. Listen in silence. Journal what came up for you from the meditation.

Solitude

'We enter solitude in which we also lose loneliness. True solitude is found in the wild places, where one is without human obligation. One's inner voices become audible… In consequence, one responds more clearly to other lives.'

Wendell Berry[1]

In solitude we can remember who we are.

Solitude is not to be confused with loneliness. Solitude is a luxurious state that gives us the quiet spaciousness to develop a closer intimacy with ourselves and with the unknown.

Yet often we find ourselves reluctant and fearful to seek out solitude for ourselves. We are afraid of our chattering monkey minds, afraid of finding out what we really feel and think, afraid of touching our rawness, hurts and vulnerabilities, afraid of our awkwardness in our aloneness, memories of being abandoned or forgotten… But once we settle, we can see new patterns in the weave, a new richness and a new dimension to our evolving inner life which can delight, empower and surprise us.

This is because solitude is a place where the repertoire of 'musts' and 'shoulds' – both our own and other people's – cease to ring in our ears. In solitude we can drop our masks and shed our outer skins to live into our vulnerabilities. Here we can stop telling ourselves the stories which are trapping us or boring us – and can dare to re-imagine new storylines.

In our solitude we can sense into the deeper webs of connection where our own patterns and those of life can be more fully experienced. Solitude enables us to fully live in our bodies as a question rather than as an answer to other people's questions.

In our solitude we pull back the veil and step in a deeper, more infinite reality, which can be both beautiful and painful. Here we can speak to the rawest and most vulnerable parts of ourselves and also to our dreams and to our creativity. Here we can hear our own precious wild inner voice speak. Here we can find our balance and the ground from which we step forward.

Enjoying solitude can feel alien in today's plugged-in world. And we can often be lonelier in a crowd than when we give ourselves permission to be solitary – if even for a short while. We do not have to be hermits to be in regular contact with our solitude. Nor do we have to banish ourselves or feel that we need to go into long periods of solitary confinement to find the resourcing companionship of befriending ourselves. We can simply find moments of retreat and solitude – places of refuge where we can calm our sensory overload and spark our creativity. Periods of solitude can bring us back in to a right (or better) relationship with ourselves and the world. The risk is that if we experience more solitude than we can healthily tolerate we can find ourselves either ruminating or disengaging.

When we sit in solitude, we can hear our hearts beat, hear our breath and hear ourselves think without censorship. We can tune into our own music and our own rhythm. In solitude we can get back on track.

Songlines

Invitation: 'A Day Off'

Maya Angelou used to say that we needed to take at least one day a year when we can be completely alone. And so, with this in mind, diary a day when you know you can be completely alone – or where you are able to keep contact with other people to a minimum. Get your supplies of food and drinks in. Switch off your social media feeds. Give yourself a question that you want to consider. Make a gentle plan about how you want to spend your day. If you feel a wave of loneliness – or the fear of loneliness – rising within you just embrace and soothe it as you embrace your solitude practice.

A Journaling Practice

Reflect on your own relationship with solitude. What is the difference for you between loneliness and solitude – and does this play out in your life? How can you better befriend solitude? How can you reclaim your solitude? When for you does solitude become disengagement and withdrawal? What is the balance for you between solitude and being in community?

Start

'Vision is not enough; it must be combined with venture.

It is not enough to stare up the steps, we must step up the stairs.'

Victor Havel[1]

Start from where you are.

Just starting or stopping something can be the biggest step we do not want to take.

Each of us has our own relationship with starting something new or starting the end of something. Stopping can also be a new start.

There is an art to starting. Getting ready holds the key. How we ready ourselves is the work before the work. We are required to be ready. Jumping too soon might mean we have not done the work before the work. A reluctance to start can look like procrastination, but it may be necessary for the processes of germination, when ideas are still forming and are too tender to yet appear. Hibernation and germination can be necessary parts of getting started. Everything starts life in the dark. At its best, starting is a declaration that the germination process is complete.

Homecomings

Starting is hard because it requires us to move out of our comfort zone to step into some unknown, where we are not sure how things will play out. Starting brings forth the anxieties and fears that have lain conveniently hidden or dormant – our fears of being seen, of not being good enough, of not being equal to the task, of looking foolish, of compromising, of not completing, of suffering loss by committing to one path.

It means that we begin to risk ourselves – we become visible and exposed in new and different ways as we commit. Our shadows and our scripts start stirring. Our head brain pulls us back, thinking of all the things that could 'go wrong' in an attempt to keep us safe and in control of the steady state. This is an inner tussle between our head, our heart and our soul to move beyond 'what is' into bigger wider spaces – an ancient evolutionary battle between the need to just survive and our desire to thrive and to flourish. Our head brain is suspicious of imaginative leaps because it works in the linear language of facts, evidence and rationality, rather than in the language of symbols, imagination, visions and dreams.

Starting can also mean a moving on and a letting go of what was, marking the end of something – be it a home, a relationship, a dream, an identity, or a life. Starting can also mean choosing with the foreclosing of other options which held life and possibility – if even for a short time. As we journey through life, we can forget to honour our goodbyes – to grieve for what we have had to let go of – as much as welcome our new 'hellos'.

Delaying tactics and lethargy set in, giving reasons to stay put. Our inner critic or editor runs amok, giving us all the reasons to stay small and to play it safe – to leave 'it' to another person or for another day. It is scary because when we commit ourselves, we are making a promise. We think we need to know the 'end point' – and all the steps in-between – and forget to trust that the path unfolds and reveals itself once we make our vows, set our intention and commit.

Starting in small micro ways gives us a chance to test our ideas and receive the feedforward we need to craft out next steps. We learn through our doing. In our need for control, we forget that every start needs to be approached with a beginner's mindset. We also forget that starting is an act of courage. The stem of 'courage' is 'coeur' which is 'heart' in French – so starting is the work of the heart. And when we dare to commit, both visible and invisible help seems to arrive. It is as if the universe is encouraging and resourcing us in our endeavours.

The curious part of us is wired for growth and adventure, because if we do not grow, we are just standing still like the frog in the boiling saucepan who gets so comfortable it does not realize when the water has become too hot and it is time to jump.

Rather than being forced into starting by external forces, let us start because the wisest part of ourselves feels that it is right to do so.

Songlines

Invitation: Tuning In

We often forget that the key to getting started is getting ready – the work before the work. Readiness is a felt sense which resides deep within our bodies – like a bulb which finally pushes through the soil when the conditions are right. This invites us to pay attention to both the bedrock practices which sustain us over the long haul to hone our readiness and our in-motion reflections which keep us on point in the moment.

Where in your body do you feel the urge to start? Notice the sensation. What does it feel like? What is wanting to move or shift within you? As you start, (whatever you are starting) notice who you are becoming and notice the feedforward or reactions of others. Remember that this is all data (and it is not necessarily personal). Become your own research project.

A Journaling Practice

How easy is it for you to start and to take the first step? How can you ready yourself – what is your work before the work? How can you become more 'artful' in your starting? When do you procrastinate and when do you commit? What is your 'YES'? As you journal really tune into what you are noticing, what you are feeling, what you are learning and what is now needed from you?

Safety

'Feelings of worth can flourish only in an atmosphere where individual differences are appreciated, mistakes are tolerated, communication is open and rules are flexible – the kind of atmosphere that is found in a nurturing family.'

Virginia Satir[1]

Feeling safe is paradoxically the precursor to adventure, experimentation and discovery.

Feeling safe and secure is a primal need. It is a precursor to building and maintaining trust – in the people around us and for the world. Feeling safe is a necessary condition for development – for how we play, how we explore our work, and how we risk ourselves as we learn and grow.

As babies we are shaped by our sense of feeling safe. Babies are helpless and need the basic requirements of food, warmth, love and care. This in turn enables us as babies – when we are so very vulnerable and dependent – to build healthy and secure attachments to our care givers – where our needs will be met with appropriate and timely sensitivity. If babies do not experience this, they can develop patterns of insecure,

anxious or avoidant behaviour which, in turn, can inhibit their capacity to learn, trust and take risks as they mature[2].

We are hardwired to seek out safety. Our own sense of safety sits in the primitive part of our brain. It was useful when we were hunter-gatherers, where the rapid detection of threats was literally a matter of life and death. However, today luckily for most of us these threats are not a daily reality, but our brains can still act as if this were so. This hypervigilance and reactivity can get in the way of our ability to be fully present to the joy of what is, can stall our relationships and can put the brakes on our curiosity and learning.

Feeling safe is a completely personal state and dependent upon the changing situations and contexts that we find ourselves in. People are triggered and mollified by different things, depending on their history, their experiences and their personal make-up as well as often their sense that they are being criticised or judged.

Feeling safe is often experienced as an unnamed felt sense, which arrives in our emotional body, often through our multiple levels of sensory scanning on the lookout for potential threats. Safety is sometimes easier to spot by its absence than by its presence. When it is absent, we find ourselves experiencing the need to either fight, fly, freeze or flop – a rolling up or a contraction to protect, to preserve and to survive.

It is not only a sense of physical safety but a psychological, emotional and social safety that we seek. We need to feel appreciatively and unconditionally accepted. Safety is not automatic or guaranteed – it has to be co-created, tested and then sustained by lots of baby steps. And perhaps safety should start as a deep bow of respect to the other, where both parties in the relationship can feel seen and valued for who they are – with a sense of being welcomed without fear of judgment or rejection.

It is only from this place of security that we can dare to risk ourselves to explore the edges of our world.

We cannot command safety into being but as adults we can create the conditions for a feeling of safety to arrive. Understanding – and then co-creating – the preconditions that we need in any endeavour or relationship is a sign of maturity and a gateway to performance.

Songlines

Invitation: Safety First

This practice helps you to tune into times in the future when you might be feeling unsafe which always starts in your body.

Ground and centre yourself. Go back to a time when you remember feeling safe. Notice the effects that this memory is having on your body. Now tune into a time when you did not feel safe. Notice the effects that this memory is having on your body. Then shake off this memory and bring yourself back to centre. Now tune into a time when you felt extra safe. Notice the effects that this memory is having on your body. Then shake off this memory and bring yourself back to centre. Now journal or draw what you noticed and lean into what you might need to now ask of yourself and from others.

A Journaling Practice

Do you consciously create safety for yourself? Is safety a precursor for trust for you, or vice versa? Or do they advance in a dance together for you? How do you sabotage your own sense of safety? How do you create loving safety for yourself and for others?

Senses

'The senses, being explorers in the world, open us up to new knowledge.'

Maria Montessori[1]

Our senses open us up to the full experience of being alive.

For many of us the memory of a beautiful sunset, the smell of a perfume, hearing the words of a song, the touch of a fabric or the taste of a forbidden fruit is the 'kinaesthetic' or sensory/bodily backdrop to our lives, infusing us with memory, colour, rootedness, belonging and connection. And of course, what touches one person might leave another unmoved. Our sensing determines what we choose to notice and pay attention to, which in turn shapes how we are in the world.

As hunter-gatherers our finely tuned senses were the key to our survival. But, more recently in our evolution they have become at best taken for granted and at worst neglected. Our sensuality has got belittled or pushed to one side by the older puritanical dictates of the need for productivity, prudence and propriety.

Often, we criticize others for their myopia, deafness, tastelessness, odour or insensitivity, and do not see it in ourselves. But the good news is that

our senses are ready and waiting to be enlisted by us at any moment, offering us a feast or a palette of wonder which is always available to ground us, and to infuse and inspire us. Our senses are a portal to awe – or just peace.

Senses wake us up to the joy of being right here right now.

When we dare to sense into the bigger field in the present moment, boundaries of ego dissolve. In the present moment we are free to sense into what we experience, to listen deeply, and to allow life to make itself known through us, in a glorious generative act of emergence and co-creation.

'Presencing' is a verb coined by Otto Scharmer to blend 'sensing' with 'presence' to describe this phenomenon[2]. It means 'to be present to' and 'to sense into' what is wanting to emerge – to intuit what life is asking of us. It is often said that the sensing and sensory body is intelligent, knows first and keeps the score[3]. What might become possible if we dare to lean into our body's sensing intelligence and wisdom?

So stargaze, feel the wind on your face, dance barefoot on the grass, swim in a lake, pause to admire the beauty of a rose or feel the touch of the soil. Stop to listen to a piece of music resonating within you or smell the delicious aroma of spices blending in the cooking pot.

Your senses and your soul will thank you for it.

Songlines

Invitation: Waking Up your Senses.

Befriend each of your senses. You might have a favourite but enlist all five. For Listening perhaps listen to birdsong, the same piece of music through different interpretations or just sit in silence. For Seeing, really study a view, or look at the colours of everyday objects in different lights, or look for different shapes in your surroundings. For Smell, really smell the food you prepare or go outside and smell the air just after it has rained. For Touch really allow your fingers and hands to dwell on the shape and feel of objects – perhaps even with your eyes closed. And for Taste, take time to really savour the different tastes and textures of your food and drink.

A Journaling Practice

Become a detective. Find everyday objects, a view or things in nature and really study them using all of your five senses. Write about your chosen object from the perspective of each of your five senses. Write down what you now appreciate about your object, your different ways of relating to it and what you might now appreciate about it that you did not before. This journaling practice can also be extended, to wonder how your object came to be, how it was shaped and what its future might hold.

Soul

'Your soul knows the geography of your destiny. Your soul alone has the map of your future; therefore, you can trust this indirect, oblique side of yourself. If you do, it will take you where you need to go, but more important it will teach you a kindness of rhythm in your journey.'

John O'Donohue[1]

Our soul's work is to wake us up and bring us home to ourselves.

Our souls speak quietly to us in the language of dreams, symbols, metaphor, mystery, nature, poetry and music, and we need to be still and silent to hear its murmurings. Our souls are the eternal, immutable, unalterable and immaterial part of us – the part of us which makes us aware, alive and awake, and defines the essence of our personhood. Some say it lives on after our death.

Our souls hold the ancient memory and sacred mystery of who we are and why we are here[2]. Our souls connect us to the pain, the mystery, the beauty and the magic of life, helping us to see beyond the petty demands of our egos and the everyday to reach for grace, beauty, generosity,

gratitude, kindness, connection, compassion and joy to live well in the midst of all that is happening around us. Our creative expression is our own unique soul print or own unique DNA made visible in this world and is what remains of us when we die.

Our souls connect us to our shared humanity, and awaken us to the wonder of our earth, and to the immense privilege and fragile preciousness of life. Befriending our soul is a lifetime's work. Our soul work is to wake ourselves up to our inheritance so that we can honour where we came from, who we are and who we are becoming. This makes us good ancestors for future generations, as well as good citizens for the present. And, when our souls stir and awaken, we can never go back. Intimations of what lies beyond make us curious and urgent, impatient and unsatisfied now by the lowlands of the life we knew before.

Our soul is our home and our sanctuary, always there and always available to us whenever we choose to tune in – a quiet and constant compass and companion reminding us who we are and who we are becoming. Our soul reminds us that we are never alone. We can forget or abandon our soul in our busyness or lostness, but our soul never abandons us.

If we are not listening, our souls will let us know through feelings of unease or anxiety – and sometimes with low mood or depression – that we are straying from our essence and what feels true for us. Our soul also needs our nurturing and our hospitality. It also needs us to be generous hosts enabling the stillness and quiet to be heard.

When we live and lead from our souls, we are our fullest freest selves, courageously living into our true potential and wisely offering our gifts in the world, with care, generosity, compassion and wisdom.

Songlines

Invitation: Walking or Writing a Labyrinth

Labyrinths are walking, writing, or tracing meditations which are paths of prayer, mirrors for our souls, and crucibles for healing and change. The labyrinth is an ancient symbol used by people through the ages whose path can lead each of us to our own centre. As preparation find your local labyrinth by searching www.labryrinthlocator.com or print off a writing labyrinth from my website. You can also use a handheld labyrinth which you can walk with your fingers.

Ground and centre yourself. Before you enter the labyrinth, set the intention of befriending your soul. As you enter the labyrinth invite yourself to release any assumptions about what you will meet. At the centre – perhaps opening your arms – invite your soul to whisper to you. Images or metaphors might (or might not) arrive. When you feel ready, start to walk out of the labyrinth where you can process what has come to you. Journal or draw your experience or what you receive.

A Journaling Practice

Reflect on how and when you pay attention to your soul. How do you befriend it? When did you last hear the whisperings of your soul? What does your soul want you to know?

Self

'When we experience our own desire for transformation, we are feeling the universe evolving through us.'

Barbara Marx Hubbard[1]

When we move away from reaction and ego, we open up worlds of possibility.

We are born with the seeds of our full potential within us. The only real question is how to find the emotional, psychological, social and environmental conditions where our acorn could become a mighty oak.

'Who am I?', 'Who am I becoming?', 'What is my work?', 'What is me and not me?' and 'What is my why?' are the fundamental, foundational questions of any human life – always tantalizing, elusive and changeable. But the very act of asking the questions creates a space from which to explore whatever emerges. It is a journey and not a destination – and we are made by the process of journeying.

As we leave the cocoon of the womb, our little 'self' – our personality and our ego – must learn the cadences and tricks for our navigation in a big world[2]. We are born whole, but we can become fragmented within

ourselves as we learn what is needed – and the stories we need to tell ourselves – to navigate our childhood and 'fit into' our environment. The work of later life is to find our paths back to our own healing, integration and wholeness.

Self is forged in the relationships we have. As the African saying 'Umbunto' reminds us 'I am because you are' or, to quote Satish Kumar, 'So Hum' which means 'You are therefore I am'[3].

In our journeying, a bigger 'Self' can find the space to include, embrace and transcend all of our other parts, identities or experiences. When the big 'Self' moves away from reaction and ego to choose response and soul, we have the opportunity to remove ourselves from the myopic prison of 'little me' into the realm of a 'bigger me in we'.

Then the soul moves to the beat of a different drum – to a rhythm which dwells in possibility and to the eternal qualities of tenderness, grace, beauty, connection, compassion and love. When we work from the core of our bigger or higher 'Self', new vistas of potential, possibility and perspective open up, through direct experience in the moment. This embracing of the little 'self' within the home of the bigger 'Self' is possible for every one of us. Rather like Lucy in *The Lion, The Witch and the Wardrobe* when she steps through the back of the wardrobe, we can access other worlds[4]. The journey from our egocentric, dualist and defended little 'self' to our bigger 'Self' is a profound, ever unfurling spiritual journey to the elegant, naked centre of who we truly are.

Songlines

Meditation: 'What is it that remains?'

The 13th-century mystic Meister Eckhart posed the question 'What is it that remains?' His answer was, 'That which is inborn in me remains.'

Meditate on this simple but profound statement. You may want to revisit it many times. Ask yourself 'What do I need to let go of, as well as welcome?' Sense into your body's feelings when you ask Meister Eckhart's question – even asking the different parts of your body the same question and seeing what – if anything – comes up for you.

A Journaling Practice

What is your 'come from' place? How do your little 'self' and bigger 'Self' relate to each other? Are they aware of each other's existence? Is it a befriending or a battleground for you? Where are the places of fragmentation and where are the points of integration? What places need some healing or some tender loving care to come into a more wholesome wholeness?

Soul Friends

'A friend is a loved one who awakens your life in order to free the wild possibilities within you.'

John O'Donohue[1]

Our soul friends are those rare and special people who can truly 'see' us and lovingly accompany us on our untidy journey.

Friendship is a creative and subversive force. It can give us grace and strength. It can help welcome the inner artist to our journey of becoming. It may enable the unknown, anonymous, negative and obscure to reveal their secrets to us, in order that we might learn lessons from them.

To live a soulful life means to embrace both the beauty and the ache of our complex vulnerability and brilliance. Somehow, for fulfilment, balance must be found between our interior and exterior, the visible and invisible, the known and the unknown, the temporal and eternal, and the ancient and new. It is a journey of unfurling and becoming. This requires courage. Courage comes from the French word 'coeur' meaning 'heart'. It is the work of the heart. And working with the mysterious, the intimate and the unknown is a radical – and often uneasy – act of love in all its forms. Only certain special people, called soul friends, can support us in both the mystery and the struggle.

According to Celtic tradition, our soul shines around us like a luminous cloud. When we are able to be open, appreciative and trusting of another person, according to the Celts our two souls flow together. In Celtic, 'Anam' is the word for 'soul' and 'cara' means 'friend'. An 'Anam Cara' is therefore 'a soul friend' or a 'friend of your soul'. An 'Anam Cara' (or 'Caras') can bear witness: encouraging us, holding us when we fall, and resourcing us.

Your Anam Cara holds your light and beauty, sees you for who you truly are and awakens you to the mystery and fullness of your life[2]. All the possibilities of our human destiny are asleep in our soul. Our 'Anam Caras' can help us creatively to awaken our own possibilities – helping us to find our own rhythms with life. In this way, friendship can be a radicalizing force. This is often friendship felt as a deep act of anchoring, recognition and belonging. If we are lucky, it can also enable us to encounter and befriend our own experiences without feeling unseen or alone. This is the kind of friendship which is not diminished by separation or distance.

Songlines

Practice: Celebrating your Anam Caras

Get your journal, coloured pens and watercolour paints if you have any. You could paint a watercolour wash over the page of your journal. When the paint is dry, turn your journal sideways and at the centre of the page bottom, draw a small semi-circle. Draw lines out from the semi-circle like rays from the sun. Now, on each of the 'rays', write the name of a person in your life – alive or dead – who is or has been your anam cara. Then, in your journal, write a Letter of Gratitude to each of them celebrating your special friendship, what it means to you and what you might give them in return.

A Journaling Practice

Who are your anam caras? What is the difference for you between an acquaintance, a friend and a soul friend?

States of Being

'There is an ecstasy that marks the summit of life, and beyond which life cannot rise. And such is the paradox of living, this ecstasy comes when one is most alive, and it comes as a complete forgetfulness that one is alive.'

Jack London[1]

Our state of being is created by our intention and where we choose to place our attention.

A state of being is the quality of our experience in the moment and can be transitory, lasting only moments or can extend over hours or even days. Our being is more important that our doing because our being always informs our doing. Who we are is how we show up in all aspects of our lives.

When we intentionally work from a place of love – rather than fear – we find our hearts opening as we become fully present. The commitment that love brings, invites us into presence, connection, compassion and concentration because we are intentionally and completely attending to the person or the work we are engaging with. These are all qualities which support our flow or flow state. A flow state is where we can be so present, so connected and so absorbed in something without distraction that we find ourselves naturally responding to a different resonance and vibration which speaks to our soul. Here we feel both empty and full at the same time, as we become channels and open ourselves up to what is wanting to emerge through us – and only us.

And when we are fully present, there is nowhere else to go and nowhere else to be. We find freedom as we touch all of life's potential. Here there is only connection and receiving. Our boundaries dissolve as we feel ourselves fusing with energies beyond ourselves – where we move from 'I' to 'we' and to 'us'. Here we are fully awake and alive. Here we are fully aware and experience the expansion of our consciousness. Here our minds and our hearts are open, ready to co-create – to channel what wants to emerge. This is perhaps the nearest we get to being truly happy, in a natural state of grace or a state of bliss.

But when we find our state is informed by a bedrock of fear in any of its guises, we absent ourselves from the present and find ourselves functioning from places of criticism, cynicism or judgement. Here our fearful inner critic is in play, and frustrating distractions, rigid boundaries and brick walls are set up like an obstacle course to constrain and interrupt our creativity.

We cannot command ourselves into states of flow, but we can create the preconditions for it. Setting up our sanctuaries, finding stillness, scheduling time and designing our own rituals make it more likely for us enter into our flow. When we create from this place, we are finding our own true voice and the unique expression of our soul.

Songlines

Early Morning Practice: The Marriage of Intention and Attention

Centre and ground yourself. Breathe gently. Ask your heart to set its intention for the day. When this has arrived then ask your heart how it would like your newly formed intention to shape what you pay attention to and where you place your energies to during the day. Journal what has emerged for you. Then set your alarm at regular intervals or at least once during the morning, the afternoon and in the evening to self compassionately check in with yourself. How is your being influencing your doing during the day? What might have pulled you off course? If you did, how and when did you find yourself in a state of flow? What is the relationship between what you intended and where your energy flowed? Notice what is moving or shifting in you. Try again the next day as you experiment with finding your own alignment and your own way of being and doing.

A Journaling Practice

Think back to times when you felt in a state of flow. Write about each scenario. What happened? What were the preconditions or precursors for it? What did it feel like? What was possible – or not possible? What did you create? Now stand back and write what you have learnt from observing yourself and what you can now gift yourself.

Sacred

'The sacred cannot be precisely defined. Each of us perceives it through the lens of a unique personal history. For me, sacredness is an experience of the inner radiance of life, the unseen force that transforms and nourishes the physical world but is never limited by it. There is something more to it, a mystery that is never totally grasped.'

Anthony Lawlor[1]

When we tend to our souls, we touch the sacred.

Our souls are shy and need gentle care and nourishment. They need to be hosted in special places, spaces and with ceremony and ritual so that the sacred and the divine can be welcomed. Here the veil can be pierced, lifted and the sacredness of both the ordinary and extraordinary can be experienced – and here we can be nourished by remembering that awe, reverence, magic, mystery and the miraculous are just a breath away, putting our own small lives into a much bigger context. Here we can find a bliss – an ease and a grace – that brings us into oneness with ourselves and with life. The amazing thing is that anywhere can be sacred ground for us if we have eyes to see it.

Homecomings

How can we make our souls feel safe to emerge? How can we make the small scared parts of us become sacred? Creating a raft of creative reflective practices can support us. This establishes the beautiful preconditions, the hospitable spaces, and the welcoming invitation for our souls to peek out. These can include making time to journal regularly, being still, developing a mindfulness practice, taking a walk in nature, going on an Artist's Date, lighting a candle, creating a sanctuary in your home or workplace, working with a soul friend or colleague. There is no blueprint and no one way.

However, daring to create these sacred times and spaces for ourselves for connection is still a radical act of defiance and rebellion for many of us. This is because these are places and times of the day when we can escape and remove ourselves from the busy everyday into the quieter stillness where we can learn to hear all that is sacred within us and around us. This is us finding our way home in the liminal luminous sacred in-between spaces where we can commune with the transcendent away from crashing noise, frantic busyness and squeezed schedules.

Making these times special, inviolable, and sacrosanct helps us to drink from a different well – to both surrender to, and commune with, the webs of our interrelatedness and that of all things, our intuitions of wholeness and our desires for hope and healing. Our souls can be seen as the sacred feminine energy in what has become a predominately masculine world – and her wisdom is needed now more than ever.

Songlines

Invitation: Getting in Touch with the Sacred

Ground and settle yourself. Close your eyes. Bring to heart and mind the last experience of the sacred you had – when the veil between the everyday and sublime was lifted, and you stepped through. It might be a moment with another, a sunset or a sunrise, a child's smile, a place in nature, a piece of music, a poem. Step back into the experience and feel into all its sensations, colours, textures, music and sound. Enjoy your visualization. Embrace the memory. And when you open your eyes, draw or write what you experienced. Repeat this practice as often as you can to capture memories of the sacred to add to your self-care kit.

A Journaling Practice

What does sacred mean for you? How can you create the pre-conditions – the sacred spaces and places for your own wild soul to safely emerge? How can you offer safe and sacred spaces in your life and work for others?

'The love in me salutes the love in you.'

Marianne Williamson[1]

When we salute we remember to honour ourselves as well as the other.

This is an invitation to reclaim an ancient practice.

A salute can be expressed in many forms and is a respectful gesture of greeting or farewell – but it is also a lot more than this. Perhaps traditionally associated with hierarchy and the military, the democratization of 'saluting' can be a radical gesture of acknowledgement, goodwill, courtesy, respect, reciprocity and gratitude. The word 'Namaste' is increasingly used beyond the Hindu tradition as a polite and respectful greeting or farewell, and literally means 'I humbly bow to you', 'the divine in me bows to the divine in you' or 'the spirit in me honours the spirit in you'. 'Namaste' is used to acknowledge the equality between us and honours the sacredness in us all. 'Namaste' can be used at any time of the day and in any situation.

Receiving an apparently simple gesture of welcome and/or farewell is a profound and significant act of being seen and seeing another. Being saluted can be very grounding and can anchor us in our own belonging. Saluting is a deep acknowledgement and honouring of the other. What we salute in others can also be what we want to salute in ourselves.

What is possible if we make 'saluting' – whatever the format or body gesture – an opening or moment in time to pause and consciously celebrate the person or work of another? In this way we acknowledge the work of others and our sacred webs of interconnection and interrelatedness. As Maria Rainer Rilke put it: 'Praise the whole thing.'[2]

Songlines

Invitation: Saluting Salutations

Ground and centre yourself. Think back to a time when you were last saluted or expressed your respect in some way. What did it feel like? How did you behave? Now, using whatever gesture feels right for you, silently salute a person or place for the gifts that they have given you. When you have completed this, give yourself a bow – and perhaps journal your experience of this practice.

A Journaling Practice

How do you salute? How do you celebrate the feats of others as well we as yourself? How do you feedforward? How might you better open up spaces of generous welcoming and hospitality with everyday salutations? Research the different salutations which are used in different cultures across the world – and what could you model for yourself?

Footprints

'The journey is my home.'

Muriel Rukeyser

1. Seasons
2. Savour
3. 'Seeing' Another
4. Soften
5. Sadness
6. Surrender
7. Shadow
8. Suffering
9. Stagnation
10. Shape
11. Stories
12. Shame
13. Sublime
14. Seeking
15. Serendipity
16. Scanning
17. Symbols and Sideways Thinking
18. Surprise
19. Simplicity
20. Silliness
21. Souvenir

Seasons

'Study Nature.
Love Nature.
Stay close to Nature.
It will never fail you.'

Frank Lloyd Wright[1]

The Seasons offer us a mirror and a lens.

The Seasons – like our lives – imperceptibly blend and merge like an ever-turning kaleidoscope shaking up the tones, hues, light and design of the scenes before us. If we pay careful enough attention, each day offers something new or different, which is being reshaped, or which cries out for our wonderment.

And so, in the beauty, creativity, vulnerability, fragility, determination and fierceness of nature we see ourselves reflected back. Our task is often simply to catch up with ourselves and with the life that is happening within us and around us. We can use the metaphor, mirror, lens and language of nature and the changing seasons to appreciate where we are with any given issue or project. And as we learn to befriend nature, we can learn to find a solace, a comfort, a healing, and a never-ending source of inspiration that is available to us at any time, if we can just step out of the front door and dress appropriately for the weather.

As in nature, so in life. The changing seasons mirror the changing phases of any human life. Inspired by Chinese tradition, which acknowledges the season of 'late summer', we can work with five seasons (instead of four) to chart the reassuringly cyclical rhythms of nature in the northern hemisphere. And so, we can use the metaphor of the seasons to both reflect and map our own lives. Spring's tender shoots can be associated with new life and creativity, summer's blooming with flourishing and passion, late summer's mellow golds with gathering in and savouring, Autumn's russet leaves with letting go and winter's bracing cold with retreat and hibernation[2].

And as with nature so with the arc of a human life as we encounter the joy of birth and playfulness of youth and adolescence; the vibrancy of early adult live; the full richness and maturation of mid-life; and the gentler wisdom of eldership and then final release with death and return to the earth. We are embedded in the miraculous and infinite natural cycle of birth, death, and rebirth.

Songlines

Invitation: Take a Walk in Nature

This could be a year's practice cycling through the seasons.

Take time to tune into the five seasons of spring, summer, late summer, autumn and winter. Or perhaps into the Celtic calendar which marks the winter and summer solstices and the spring and autumn equinoxes and the midpoints in-between like Imbolc on the 1st and 2nd of February; Beltane on the 1st May; Lughnasadh on the 1st August and Samhain on the 1st November. Or even the 72 Japanese microclimates[3].

Take a slow and mindful walk in nature at the start of each new season. Allow yourself to become completely immersed in your surroundings. Merge into them so that you feel a part of nature and no longer separate from it or outside it. Use all five senses to really tune into the birds and wildlife; touch the bark of a tree and a leaf and feel your feet on the earth; see the panoply of colours, forms and shapes all around you; smell the scents; taste the air as you breathe. Notice what changes each time you visit from day to day, and from season to season.

Design a small ritual to mark the passing of the seasons with its lessons and gifts for us or make an Earth Altar of fragments of nature like leaves, petals, twigs or feathers that have fallen to the ground or stones that you have found.

A Journaling Practice

What is your relationship with nature? Do you see yourself as a part of nature, reflected in nature and her changing seasons or separate from it?

Savour

'I do not want to get to the end of my life to find I just lived the length of it. I want to have lived the width of it as well.'

Diane Ackerman[1]

If we could only remember to savour every moment, we would always be in celebratory awe of life's miraculous beauty and boundless generosity.

Savouring is more than appreciation. To savour we experience 'the full taste of' whereas appreciation is 'to know the value of'[2].

Savouring is an invitation to slow down, to linger, to pause and to take time to enjoy people, things, moments and nature as if we are seeing, tasting and enjoying them fully for the first time. Savouring is about paying deliberate attention – about squeezing all the juices out of every moment. This allows us not only to acknowledge, celebrate and treasure experiences in the present but to draw from them in harder times. This makes savouring a practical life skill rather than an indulgence.

Savouring reminds us of the perhaps superficially simple – but profound – pleasures of life, which we can all too easily take for granted: the smell

of a morning cup of coffee, the juiciness of a strawberry, the fragrance of a flower or lawn freshly mowed, the exquisite colours of a sunset, or the beauty of a child's smile. It also encompasses the bigger pleasures of a piece of work well done, a qualification achieved or a garden re-landscaped. Savouring is 'simple' in its purest form, made beautiful also by its fragility. It is a poignant – if not aching – reminder that life in all of its forms is transient.

Savouring serves to remind us of life's bounty, generosity and abundance. It enables us to find the wonder in the ordinary. Savouring is a counterpoint to a deficit or scarcity mindset scanning for what is missing, lacking or not there. Savouring helps us to build a bank of memories that we can draw up on when we touch into moments of loss or sadness.

In our performance-driven culture perhaps we can transform feedback into feedforward with an invitation to better savour and bottle what has been achieved. Perhaps with more savouring we can learn to love the spirit and beauty of all that is around us instead of focusing on what is lacking or missing. Savouring can help us to enjoy the harvest of our endeavours. Too often we skip past what we have built in order to lean into the next challenge or climb the next mountain. Remembering to stop and savour helps us to appreciate how far we have come.

It is a thankfulness and gratitude practice which can support our emotional and psychological wellbeing, as it also feeds our reservoirs of resilience and hope.

Songlines

Invitation: Savouring your Savouring

Savouring is in essence a mindfulness practice. Building moments of savouring into your routine can nurture and resource you. From the following list find what works for you or use it as a launchpad to design your own: savour the memories evoked by a picture or photograph, savour a memory, capture and freeze frame a special moment in your day, make a point of showing someone your appreciation of what they did for you or how they made you feel, savour each mouthful of food, feast your eyes on what you see on your walk or when you look outside your window, wonder at the colours which surround you, find five words that describe for example a glass of wine or a piece of art, create a photo montage of the ordinary in the extraordinary or jot memories down on small pieces of paper and collect them in a 'Savour Jar' or in a scrapbook which you can return to again and again.

A Journaling Practice

How could the joy of savouring become a more intentional practice for you? Sketch a store cupboard and fill the shelves with all the things that you would like to savour – like your favourite drink, a poem, a photograph, a playlist, your muses, or a special memory. Then write about how you might be able to preserve and conserve these special things or moments in your store cupboard to draw upon both for inspiration and in harder times. And can you restock and refill it as you go?

'Seeing' Another

'I see you.
I see your strength and courage, your hesitations, and fears.
I see the way you love others, and your struggle to love yourself.
I see how hard you work to grow, and your dedication to heal.
I see your vulnerable humanity, and your transcendent divinity.
I see you, and I love what I see.'

Scott Stabile[1]

I am because you are.

There are two beautiful greetings in Zulu which celebrate and confirm our shared humanity and inter-relatedness.

People greet each other with the word 'Sawubona' — literally, 'I see you; you are important to me, and I value you.' And the other replies with the word 'Shiboka' or, 'I exist for you.'

This simple return captures the heart and soul of our inter-being. It expresses an intention to put love and unconditional acceptance into the heart of social discourse. This simple but profound utterance already sows the seeds for trust to develop and points to a path of loving interrelatedness and connection from which the conversation can unfurl.

The word 'Ubuntu' means 'I Am Because You Are' and expresses the idea that humans cannot exist in isolation, and we cannot be without each other. This also speaks to the Buddhist story of Indra's Net. It is written that the great god Indra hung a huge net of silk threads over his palace which spread to infinity in all directions to establish the foundations of the world in heaven. And in each knot, he placed a precious gem which reflected all the other gems that cover the net to represent our inter-being – that everything that exists and everything that has ever existed exists and is reflected within us.[2]

Both sayings remind us that we see ourselves – and see another – through the gifts of our exquisite attention and relational presence which cost us nothing (except perhaps the quietening of our ego) but mean everything.

They also invite us into a generous reciprocity when we are reminded again and again in the words of the poet John Donne 'No man is an island entire of itself.'[3]

Songlines

Invitation: Seeing Another

Try this in pairs. Sit opposite each other. With your eyes closed or looking down, ground and centre as you connect with yourselves, noticing your in-breath as you inhale and your out-breath as you exhale. Now gradually open your eyes and become gently aware of the other person but do not make any social gestures or meet their eyes. Just let yourself be there. Now you may let yourself connect with your eyes and just notice what is happening when we are in relational presence with this other person. Now, you can smile, nod, or speak with each other. And then share what the experience felt like.

A Journaling Practice

What shifts and what becomes possible in you (and others) if we start each piece of work with the reciprocal Zulu greeting of 'Sawubona' and 'Shiboka'? What becomes possible if we allow ourselves to be guided by the insight and invitation offered to us by the word 'Ubuntu' and the story of Indra's Net?

Soften

'What actually sustains us, what is fundamentally beautiful, is compassion – for yourself and for those around you. That kind of beauty inflames the heart and enchants the soul.'

Lupita Nyong'O[1]

When we soften we can find a gentler intelligence.

Many times we can find we are holding ourselves – like granite – rigid and immobile. While we are unable to move, we stare straight ahead – fearful and busy. Our minds can close and our hearts can harden. When we are like this, we can feel impatient, inflexible, judgemental and critical. We can isolate ourselves. There is no time or space for us to allow in other perspectives or possibilities.

The antidote to rigidity is to soften, which is an invitation to find ways to become more gentle, kind and compassionate to ourselves and to others. We can establish a smarter, a more creative and a more imaginative intelligence to help us walk through life. When we do this, our minds open and our hearts soften, which brings forth a counterbalance to the

more dominant typically 'masculine' type yang energies within our culture and society. When we give ourselves the opportunity to blend the more 'feminine' yin energies of creativity, receiving and flow with the more 'masculine' yang energies of intention setting, direction and action, we find the sweet spot where flow meets focus across all aspects of our life and work.

Change happens not usually by big 'aha-aha' moments, but by tiny movements deep within the inner, more compassionate reaches of our hearts. These point us towards working with appreciation, gratitude and love. Compassion is the capacity to connect with ourselves, others and our shared humanity, with loving kindness as well as being prepared to be changed by that experience. It has its own intelligence which enables us to be softened and humbled by the interrelatedness of everyone and everything. Compassion offers us a softening spaciousness to be with the feelings of others while staying centred and connected to ourselves. Self-compassion is when we offer that spaciousness to ourselves.

With our softening we become more of a willow tree than a sturdy pine tree. We find we can flex and dance on the winds of change. We can see ourselves loosening the rigid grip of how we think things 'ought to' or 'should' be and go with what *is*. When the ice melts we can start to find fluidity and flow. We stop wishing for something different. We find that we can adapt and evolve more easily and freely as situations change without losing our roots. We can see through another's eyes. We can dare to loosen our boundaries without losing our sense of who we are. This softening is wise and savvy not mushy or flaccid. And this softening can embolden us rather than hold us stuck and playing small.

Songlines

Visualization: Body Movement Practice

Stand up. Ground and centre yourself. Connect to your breath. Now gently bring to mind a question or an issue which is concerning you. Do a body scan and notice the parts of you that feel rigid or tense. As you breathe into these parts, feel them become less tight or rigid – and notice how they might want you to move and what part of you wants to move first. How might your gaze soften? Ask yourself what the message is for you here – and how you might soften your approach or thinking or open your heart to the issue you are working on.

A Journaling Practice

Look back over the last week and bring to mind simple acts of kindness which you have either extended to others or received yourself from others. Journal how you felt at the time and how these acts of kindness might have loosened or softened something within you which brought about a new appreciation or insight. And ask yourself how you might open yourself up to more of this?

Sadness

'So, it is true, when all is said and done, grief is the price we pay for love.'

E. A. Bucchianeri[1]

Our times of sadness show us what and how we love.

Feeling sad is the price we pay for loving. Feeling sad is a way of honouring what we had, serving to connect us to the beauty, the preciousness, the fragility and the transitory nature of life – a tender reminder that nothing ever stays the same.

It is an inevitable part of our human condition, connecting us to our own humanity, our shared humanity and to all of life. It is a universal of human experience[2]. The only choice we have is how we choose to inhabit our sadnesses.

Our sadnesses can take many forms (sometimes several at once) and can be the result of a wide variety of circumstances: the loss of a loved one, a breakup, the loss of youth, a relinquished identity, an unfulfilled dream. Maybe we can also be sad for the planet. We are sad when we lose what

we love. Our sadnesses help us to acknowledge what we had and have much to teach us.

Sometimes our sadness can feel so sharp that we just want to repress our pain or run away from it. But the pain of sadness (if we can bear it) is the doorway into a present moment invitation to alertness, to particularity and to the possibility of healing. Our 'heavy hearts' make us humble, vulnerable and inquiring as we drop the guise of what we thought we knew to explore a new dispensation – an invitation to embrace our woundedness and our vulnerability. Can we allow ourselves to realize that our sadness needs our gentle tenderness, and our loving care for it to feel seen, included and made welcome – and is not something that needs to be excluded, denied or made to be other from us? And can we see how it is often through our vulnerabilities – rather than the sharing of our triumphs – that we can learn how to be generous and kind to ourselves? From deep sadness, the gift of self-compassion for ourselves and compassion for others can spring.

The sadnesses of any human life can also get woven into a deep sadness for the world's cruelties and tragedies. Our personal sadness can give us a fellowship with all those who struggle, giving us a bigger context in which to view our lives. 'Weltschmerz' is a German word coined by author Jean Paul in his novel *Selina*[3]. 'Weltschmerz' describes a deep connection with the pain of the world and also a weariness for the imperfections of the world.

Our news is full of injustices and tragedies. Facing into our own sadnesses and those of the wider world can make us fearful. But what would be possible for us if we knew that our hearts could be broken open without falling apart? We might become generous citizens of loss. We might, being sad, become a force for change.

And how can we become more hospitable to our own sadnesses – and the sadnesses of others? Perhaps by seeing sadness as a necessary part of a journey of honouring, celebration and letting go of something now in the past, to make way for something new to emerge.

Songlines

Invitation: Hosting Sadness

Centre and ground yourself. When you are ready, ask yourself 'Where in my body do I feel vulnerable or sad?'. Locate that part and feel into its colours and sensations. Put both hands there. Breathe into the place. Give your sadness a name or a metaphor if either suggests itself to you. Invite your sadness to sit down with you and ask it what it wants you to know – what gifts or wisdom it holds for you. Ask your sadness how you can befriend each other. Welcome it and journey together, along with all the other parts of you. Thank your sadness for what it holds for you.

Over time you can repeat this visualization for the same sadness or for different ones as you learn to become a generous host to everything that you hold.

A Journaling Practice

What would be possible for you if you knew that your heart can break open without you falling apart? What then might you be able to risk?

Surrender

'Beyond our ideas of right-doing and wrong-doing,
there is a field. I'll meet you there.
When the soul lies down in that grass,
the world is too full to talk about.
Ideas, language, even the phrase "each other"
doesn't make sense anymore.'
Rumi[1]

Surrendering is also a radical liberation, where we invite in what is wanting or needing to emerge.

Surrendering is not necessarily a capitulation or a giving up but can be a strategic withdrawal, because what we are doing or striving for is no longer working, desired or necessary. Like Sisyphus we can condemn ourselves to eternal loops of pushing against flow, gravity or against our own natures only to get the results we always get[2]. One dictionary definition of surrender is 'to yield' which feels like an invitation to 'be with' and 'work with' life's natural flows and processes[3] for new or different harvests.

In our deeper surrendering we give ourselves – sometimes reluctantly – the space and the permission to let go of what is holding us back, to open ourselves up to wider possibilities. The letting go can be scary as we leave the shores of our known lands to venture into the bigger wilder seas of re-imagining.

As we journey through life, we will encounter many mini or major surrenderings – some forced upon us and some our own choice. The only decision we have to make is how to surrender into our surrenderings – whether to dance this dance with grace or grudging resistance.

But what if we saw surrender as the first move in a beautiful dance of relaxing, releasing our grip and making space – a prelude or opening up to what wants to naturally emerge? What if we saw surrender not as a sacrifice but as a celebration of possibility and potential? What if we saw surrender as freedom to find new – and more courageous – ways of re-engaging with ourselves and the world? And what if we saw surrender as an inevitable part of any learning or change process because it allows space for the creative cycle of birth, death and re-birth?

In our surrendering we can make a conscious decision to step into the present moment and to give up, however temporarily, on the ties that bind – on our habits of trying to shape, coerce, resist, struggle or judge. To have a holiday from ourselves. We can let life find us. What can feel like being lost, is in fact life trying to find us – and from here, we can breathe fresh air into our contraction or disappearance and feel new sparks of re-emergence and expansion when the time is right. What – like Phoenix when it rose from the ashes – wants to make itself known?[4]. In our apparent surrendering we are not actually giving up, but simply letting be and saying 'yes' to life, wherever it takes us.

Songlines

Visualization: Surrender and Set Yourself Free

Ground and centre yourself. Ask your heart what thought, feeling or situation is holding you hostage and should you surrender? Hold the issue in a tightly clenched ball in your hands. Feel the tension and the weight of it. Imagine the issue as wet heavy grains of sand. Then gently breathe air and light into your hands feeling the grains get dry and lighter. Gradually spread your fingers open so that the grains of sand can fall to the floor and your hands empty, giving away what is not yours or what is no longer serving you, keeping only what is yours to work on. Then turn the palms of your hands over and feel the physical release of what was holding you hostage, allowing it to lose its power and strength bringing love, light and potential into the empty spaces. Remember this visualization when you are gripped again.

A Journaling Practice

What is your perception of surrender? How could you transform surrender into a glorious opening up and saying 'yes' to life?

Shadow

'There can be no lotus flower without the mud.'

Thich Nhat Nanh[1]

There can be no light without shadow.

The less claimed – or even denied – parts of ourselves live in our shadow. These can contain much wisdom. Our shadow is where all our uncomfortable edges reside – the home of our inner critic, our competitor, our criticizer, our moaner, our editor and our judge. Our shadow contains the vulnerable and sometime sticky revelation of who we are behind the masks we wear[2].

Wherever we go our shadow comes too. Our shadow is neither good nor bad, but merely inescapable. Our shadow does not exist by itself but is cast by the real physical presence of our body. In other words, our shadow is the unavoidable consequence of our light and of living in the world.

Our shadowlands are often detected and experienced by others before we are aware of them. Here lies the potential embarrassment of discovery and the potential gift of being seen for all we are. Every single virtue is made valid by its opposite: ying needs yang, light needs the dark, and there is no good without bad.

Our tendency is to expend massive amounts of energy ignoring or denying uncomfortable and inconvenient truths about ourselves. But to commune with and befriend these difficult, harsh and often raw parts of ourselves with gentle curiosity, love, compassion and courage holds the invitation into a more grounded and seamless wholeness as we stand in the light.

'Owning our own shadow' is often one of the mantras of a lifelong journey of personal and spiritual development. This is the practice where we can start to come home to ourselves – to re-relate or re-story our stories – an opportunity to question those stories which are no longer true or ours to own – which live in the muddy murkiness of our shadowlands. Here we can remember ourselves in the gentler light of day. No mud no lotus.

We are rarely one extreme or another, but a mixed bag of both. To befriend our shadow is to understand how to live on the shifting frontier of light and dark and learn how to inhabit both.

Songlines

Contemplation: A Zen Kaon

Work with the statement made by Carl Jung 'How can I be substantial if I do not cast a shadow? I must have a dark side if I am to be whole'. Make different body shapes in the sun on a sunny day at different times of the day. When does your body and your shadow fall into alignment and become one? Ask yourself how you might be able to welcome more of your own shadow into the light?

Homecomings

A Journaling Practice

What wisdom do your shadows hold for you? What gifts do they offer you?

Suffering

'Although the world is full of suffering. It is also full of the overcoming of it.'

Helen Keller[1]

Suffering or being able to be with another's suffering is the work of the tender loving heart.

Pain is a part of any human life. The Buddhists teach us that pain is inevitable, and that life is impermanent, but that suffering is optional. That whatever its source pain is pain – but the way that we can think about and relate to our pain can turn our pain into suffering. Pain becomes suffering when we make it so. As Buddhism puts it, pain is the first unavoidable arrow (because of injury, illness, or life events) and suffering is the second avoidable arrow. It is not so much what happens to us but how we respond that can deepen our anguish and our suffering[2].

There is no shortcut through pain. And it is in our first arrow of pain and woundedness – the crack – as Leonard Cohen writes 'that lets the light in'[3]. We do not choose pain, but we can learn to be aware of its teachings.

Buddhism offers us a bigger picture. It invites us to recognize that suffering

is the actual state of existence; that the origins of our suffering come from our cravings which cause us to behave selfishly; that our suffering ends when we realize there is no self, and we start to train our mind to live an ethical life[4]. To quote from Wei Wu Wei 'Why are you unhappy? Because 99.9 percent of everything you think, and of everything you do, is for yourself – and there isn't one.'[5]

When we can embrace the fullness of life – which contains both pain and pleasure – we can allow ourselves to be with the wholeness of what is – with all its brokenness, impermanence and imperfection. But when we encounter pain, perhaps we could turn to love which asks us to be courageously, compassionately, and lovingly present with all of what is here now, including anguish, distress and suffering. Perhaps love could help us to find our own balance point between compassion and equanimity when we encounter pain in others as well as within ourselves.

Songlines

Invitation: The Two Buddhist Arrows of Pain and Suffering

Ground and centre yourself. Breathe deeply. Locate the site of your pain. Place your hands on the site of your pain if that feels right for you. Feel your way into the purity of your pain detaching yourself from all the stories and messages which surround your pain and which turn your pain into suffering. Say to your pain 'everything is welcome'. Ask it what it needs from you right now and how you can be together right now. What act of self-compassion is needed right here, right now? Visualize the stories and messages you tell yourself – or others tell you – falling away so that you befriend and soothe your pain.

A Journaling Practice

What is your relationship with pain in all of its guises? How does pain become suffering in your experience? How might pain and suffering be eased?

Stagnation

'Life is never stagnation. It is constant movement, un-rhythmic movement, as we are in constant change. Things live by moving and gain strength as they go.'

Bruce Lee[1]

What appears to be stagnation can be life resting and readying herself.

Stagnation or 'feeling stagnant' is viewed as a bad thing. We prize busyness, but paradoxically, the busyness itself feels devoid of life-giving nutrients and nourishment.

We have learnt to fear stagnation rather than see it as a welcome part of our own natural process of change. This is because when we are feeling stagnant – which the dictionary defines as a 'state or condition, which is marked by a lack of flow, or movement' – we can feel inertia.

It could be argued that change happens when we arrange to become bored with ourselves, bored with the conversations we are having and bored by the stories we tell ourselves. Julia Cameron calls this 'overfishing'

– an 'overfishing of our inner reservoir' which empties us of inspiration and drains our own wider ecology[2].

This *ennui* is an important sign to wake up – an opportunity for us to catch up with ourselves and to notice the tender seeds of what is wanting to emerge. Wintering is a time of rest, stillness, retreat and hibernation and also of germination, as everything starts life from the inside and in the dark. And so, in our wintering there is still movement and life, albeit perhaps in the dark – slow and unseen. Even in the shedding of old skins there is a regeneration, with the composting and recycling of materials into new forms and purposes, because in nature nothing is ever wasted.

Stopping is a healthy response to stagnation. It is also a radical act of self-care – to stop and rest from doing what we have always been or done. Withdrawal into fallow periods can be the very best way of stepping forward – and a radical act of freedom.

Farming used to be based on rotating some the fields to leave some fallow for a year to allow them to recuperate and regenerate before the next season's planting. And every few years some species of tree – like the apple, oak, maple or the beech tree – produce bumper crops of seeds. These years are called 'mast years'. Other years, this is not so. Years of flourishing are followed by years of lower output, with a resting and a conserving of energy, which is needed for the trees to be able to flourish in the future. Trees need water, light, nutrients, and warmth to grow and in winter when these are in shorter supply, the sap returns to the ground and the trees become dormant to conserve energy. What looks like dormancy and stagnation is a response to the environmental conditions. It is preparation. Our own wintering mirrors the natural world as we hibernate – retreating as we take time for rest and reflection – in readiness for Spring's seeding and tending.

And so, what would be possible if we reframed the feeling of stagnation as part of our natural flow and a healthy – perhaps urgent – invitation to stop? What if we saw stagnation as a pressing request to breathe new light and air into our lives to find a new or different rhythm?

Songlines

Invitation: Finding Your Natural Rhythms

When you feel that you are stagnating, ground and centre yourself. Draw a seedbed, a fallow field and a compost bin in your journal.

Then, when you are ready, connect with the part of you which feels stuck in your body. If you are feeling safe, stay with it, feel it, touch it, see it and welcome it for the wisdom it holds. And then ask it for its wisdom – does it need your patience and some tender incubation time to find its form? Does it need to be ploughed into your fallow field where it can be parked and rest a while before you return to it? Or does it need to be put into the compost heap so it can mulch and come back in a completely different form? Or something else? Then complete your drawing and journal as you notice what is stirring within you.

A Journaling Practice

What is your relationship with stagnation? What important messages might the notion of stagnation hold for you?

Shape

'We shape our self
to fit this world
and by the world
are shaped again.
The visible
and the invisible
working together
in common cause,
to produce
the miraculous.'

David Whyte[1]

The shape we make in the world is our inner world made visible.

Our shape is defined by our bodies and the figure we make as we walk through life. And there are times when we feel that we are both physical and emotionally twisted 'out of shape' – times when we no longer recognize who we are or where we belong.

Homecomings

So often we hear people say that are 'bent out of shape' or when they look in the mirror that they 'do not recognize who they have become'. What stories or scripts or attachment patterns pull you out of shape? So often our own inner work is to 'reshape' or 'shapeshift' as we find new shapes to inhabit which better reflect our current reality. We are shaped by the world as we shape our world. To what extent and degree is this metamorphosis an elegant (and chosen) dance of becoming and when is it a contorted adaptation apparently required of us by our environment? How do we know the difference?

Our bodies are our home on earth. Our bodies define our physical arrival and advise us of our changing presence as we age. Our body also contains our sensing organs of perception. Our bodies will let us know when we are feeling curious, joyful or excited ... and when we are bored, tired, stressed or near to burnout. Our bodies keep the score, and are a repository for all our experiences and memories[2]. It could be argued that our most important ethical duty is to pay attention to what our bodies are telling us.

Much is now written to encourage us to tune into our bodies, to trust our instincts and our intuition, and to help us to heal our splitting, our upsets and also our traumas as we go through life. Mindfulness and meditation practices all help us to tune into our bodies, to trust our instincts, and to calm our systems as we try to choose a creative response rather than knee-jerk reaction when we feel misshapen. These practices remind us that there is a difference between who we really are and those transitory, fleeting feelings.

The purpose of our own developmental or spiritual journeys is to accept (and perhaps embrace) our own evolving self and shape – to retain or refine the essence of ourselves, as our external appearance changes with age. We do not get to choose if and when we are going to be taken to our edges – but we can choose to accept the invitation. Our edges are the places of our greatest vulnerabilities, and hence – if we dare to embrace them – can also be the places of greatest growth.

When we feel overwhelmed, it can seem as though the world is taking us over with its demands and we can feel diminished by this. We can experience it as a kind of shrinking or taking up less space in the world. Part of our inner work might be to stand our ground and proudly take up that space again as we feel we used to or as we have always known we could.

Songlines

Invitation: Dancing Like Nobody is Watching

Set a timer for 3 minutes. Put some dance music on and dance. Notice how your body warms up to the beat and the rhythm. Notice how your body wants to move – how it might want to stretch, centre, play, cut different shapes and express itself. When the timer goes off notice the position that your body is in. And then see which part of your body wants to imperceptibly move first. What does this part of your body want to say to you now about the shape you are in or what might need to be reshaped?

A Journaling Practice

What shape are you in? What shape shifting are you doing now? What makes your heart sing? What radical self-care do you need?

Stories

'The story that we tell
about what we must do
or be, or say,
deafens us to music
that is ours alone to play.

The story that is ours
to live completely
is a mystery to us –
because we are busy telling ourselves stories
that no longer fit –
until we wake one day
and see life with newly opened eyes,
full of surprise.'

Judy Brown 'The Story That We Tell'[1]

Stories are how we author ourselves.

We all love stories. Stories enchant us, entertain us, connect us and remind us. We are all natural story makers and pattern makers. We very naturally define ourselves by the stories we tell ourselves – and the meaning that we make from them.

Our stories sculpt us. Everything we experience becomes part of our story reel – our library and our treasure trove of everything we have seen, been, done and learnt and everything in-between. And so, we always need to be mindful. Which of our stories are contemporary and supportive and do we need to keep? Which stories have helped us but are no longer relevant, so we need to let them go? What new stories do we want to write?

The stories we tell ourselves and others can either confine us or set us free. Some are vivid, some have faded, and some are waiting to be invited back in. And much can depend on where we start in our story.

In Transactional Analysis, our stories can become the 'scripts' which can inform the decisions we live by in adult life[2]. As adults we can find ourselves acting act out our 'scripts' often unconsciously and out of our awareness with that often-familiar sinking feeling of 'here I go again'. Scripts are a natural part of our growing up, but they are not always helpful. Scripts enabled the little person we once were to find ways to adapt, to fit in and to survive in a big world but in later life they might no longer be appropriate or helpful.

For change to happen we sometimes need to wear out the stories we keep telling. We might need to re-author and re-story some of our stories. And so, the task seems to be how we can we re-write the predictable endings without whitewashing the good, the bad and the ugly; how we can learn to keep our stories fresh, alive, truthful and empowering, perhaps

even forgetting the story but taking away the lesson; and how we can avoid naming things too early – forcing a reductionist narrative shape and identity onto things before our ideas or storylines are ready. Instead of seeing ourselves as the completed novel, perhaps there is power in seeing ourselves as the empty page where a collection of short stories are in the making.

Telling our stories can be an act of remembrance. Memories are very personal and very fragile – because we see things as we are, not as the world is. In our storytelling we share something of ourselves – of what has formed, influenced and shaped us, and in our storytelling together we can bond through our shared experience and our shared humanity. When we remember we need to bear in mind that our stories hold only *our* truth, which is not the same as *the* truth or *others'* truths.

In our re-storying we can give ourselves permission to re-draft and re-author some of our own chapters – as well as write new ones – to better craft our own narratives so that we can live with ease and purpose. In this way we can learn to be more fully present in the unfolding moment which, ultimately, is all we have.

Songlines

Invitation: A 'Re-Storying' Exercise

Cut up squares of coloured paper. On each square write the title of a story which you keep telling yourself which no longer serves. Keep going until you have exhausted your memory bank. Put these titles in a pile to your left.

Now on each square write the title of the stories that you want to write or rewrite. Keep going until you have exhausted your imagination. Put these titles in a pile to your right. Compare and contrast your separate piles. Review the titles in your left-hand pile and ask yourself if there are any stories here that you would like to redraft – and if so move them to your right-hand pile. Then with your left-hand pile find a way of discarding them in some ritual as they are no longer serving you – it might for example be tearing them up and putting them in the bin or putting them in a fire or if your paper is recyclable putting them in the earth or compost heap. Refreshed, return to your right-hand pile and start your re-storying project.

A Journaling Practice

Are you bored with your own stories? Dare to dream. Who might you be or what might you be doing without this particular chapter or storyline in your life? Rewrite the story in the format of a fairy tale or fable – and how does it end? What emerges for you as you write?

Shame

'We cultivate love when we allow our most vulnerable and powerful selves to be deeply seen and known, and when we honour the spiritual connection that grows from that offering with trust, respect, kindness and affection. Love is not something we give or get; ... we can only love others as much as we love ourselves. Shame, blame, disrespect, betrayal and the withholding of affection damage the roots from which love grows. Love can only survive these injuries if they are acknowledged, healed and rare.'

Brené Brown[1]

Shame sometimes twists us, eating away at our marrow and the places where love can grow.

Shame can descend like a blanket of mist or fog obscuring our vision and reducing our room for manoeuvre. Shame seeps into the bones of who we are, tricking us into believing that we are flawed in some way — that it is something or things that we have done, could have done, or failed to do — which makes us feel unworthy of love, respect, connection and belonging. Shame in this way provokes in us a fear of rejection — of disconnection and isolation from our tribe or our community.

Shame is personal, persuasive and all-pervasive. Shame diminishes and inhibits our self-expression and our ability to show up. It creeps in and becomes part – if not all – of our identity for a long or short time. We shrink and become small – feeling a sense of 'less than' and 'not good enough' at the very core of our being.

Shame can grow from our own sense of failing and failure just as it can grow from the assumptions, actions or transgressions made against us or about us. Shame happens as we internalize our unworthiness. It can be the stories we tell ourselves – or which are told by others – which we believe. The public act of 'shaming' is what others can do to us. It is often used to control us.

Shame makes us stuck. Shame – like a trauma – puts our body into a freeze or flop state where our normal ability to think, reflect and act clearly becomes obscured, muddled and blurred. And rather than seeking balance or redress, shame immobilizes us. We can be tricked into feeling so ashamed and unworthy that we sabotage the good, our sense of agency and what is possible.

Shame is different from guilt. Guilt is related to a particular behaviour, conversation or action (or non-action) which transgressed our own values, upset another or caused harm to another. Guilt when it is functioning best, empowers us to see and to own our errors and mistakes. Guilt – when we have processed it (and possibly – hopefully – even forgiven ourselves) – may be a springboard for constructive action: to learn, to make good, to repair, to remedy errors made. Guilt means that we care. Guilt has the potential to elevate us. Shame reduces us.

Converting shame's prison sentence of unworthiness into a freedom pass of self-worth is a radical act of defiance, self-compassion and self-love. Love in all its forms can conquer shame. Shame cannot survive love. Compassion for ourselves and others can banish shame.

Songlines

Invitation: Differentiating Between Shame and Guilt

Think back to a time when you felt that were getting something 'wrong'. Describe what happened in your journal. Then draw a line down the middle page of your journal. Title the left-hand column 'Guilt' and the right-hand column 'Shame'. In the 'Guilt' column write how you felt guilty about what happened. In the right-hand column write how you felt shame about what happened. Take a short break and stand back and ask your wisest self what you could reframe here with a change in perspective, or a dose of forgiving self-compassion or compassion from others. If you remain stuck, talk about it with a friend you can trust to help you gain new perspectives.

A Journaling Practice

What is your relationship with shame and with guilt? When do you experience shame? Do you have a 'shame script'? When do you go on a 'guilt trip?' What is needed?

Sublime

'Everything has beauty, but not everyone sees it.'

Confucious[1]

Opening ourselves up to transcendence gives meaning to our lives.

Life is full of the sublime – a beauty that takes us beyond our rational selves to marvel at the sheer magic and poetic mystery of creation. When we see beauty, or grace or nobility in both the extraordinary and the ordinary, the beautiful in the ugly, the light in the dark, resilience in struggle the unfamiliar in the familiar or the comic in the tragic – we are waking up to the sublime – to a transcendent awe, mystery, majesty and wonder beyond ourselves. We are allowing ourselves to be permeable – to be opened, moved and touched by the mystery of what we encounter and what we behold. But in our busyness, we can often forget to look for the sublime – or allow it to touch us.

The sublime is everywhere if we have eyes to see it. Noticing the sublime in a smile, the smell of flowers, a tree arching into the sky, a kindness extended or a phrase in music – is a moment of pure poetry. Beauty can

stun us and take our breath away. Seeing the sublime – and being prepared to be changed or regulated by it in some way – is an act of contemplative mindfulness and joyous celebration. To paraphrase James Hillman, our souls are born in beauty, feed on beauty and require beauty for life. Beauty is a necessity and is the way that the gods touch our senses, reach our heart and attract us into life[2].

When we are full of awe, we are meeting life with a reverential honour and respect for its abundance, bounty and generosity – and also its fragility. We are enchanted. And when we are full of wonder we are meeting life with a feeling of joyous astonishment, amazement and admiration when we encounter someone or something which is beautiful or remarkable – or the beauty which walks alongside fragility, difficulty or loss. In these snatches, we experience a resonance and a connectedness with life and the universe which touches our soul. A glorious golden thread reaches out and connects us back into the very ground of our being. In our awe and wonder we are gifted anchors – reminders that life can have purpose and meaning. It is perhaps these moments which create a precious reservoir of treasured images which we can call upon when we need sustenance and nourishment. It is our human task – and our human privilege – to drink in the 'fullness' of life.

Thoughts, feelings or actions which are fed by beauty and wonder can become more compassionate, gracious and graceful. 'Hòzhò' is the Navajo Indian word for 'the Way of Beauty' or 'the Beauty Way'. 'The Way of Beauty' is a practice which cultivates living a life with beauty, balance, harmony and wellbeing at its heart[3].

Songlines

Invitation: Opening Up to Amazement

Opening ourselves up to awe and amazement invites us to really notice who and what are around us. So, take time to admire a stunning piece of art or photography, writing or music; drink in a beautiful dawn or sunset or vista near you; take time to notice the beauty of the natural world and the changing seasons around you; be ready to pause and be delighted by something you are seeing, hearing or doing, or by the relationship that you really cherish.

A Journaling Practice

Write about a time when you were astonished by the sublime. When did you last stop and stare to 'drink in' what is around you? How might you cultivate a practice which gives you a constant infusion of that which is above and beyond?

Seeking

'You must learn one thing.
The world was made to be free in.
Give up all the other worlds
except the one to which you belong.
Sometimes it takes darkness and the sweet
confinement of your aloneness
to learn
anything or anyone
that does not bring you alive
is too small for you.'

Extract from the poem 'Sweet Darkness' by David Whyte[1]

Might it be possible that what you are seeking is also seeking you?

Much of our later life is spent in a search to find our true purpose and a true sense of belonging in the world. This often comes from a deep desire to move beyond the pillars of external referencing, conformity and uniformity, to find another way which is truly our own. Or we become tired with ourselves or the stories we tell ourselves. This is in essence a spiritual journey of daring to listen to our souls calling us back to what is in our hearts[2].

Our quest for roles, qualifications, jobs and status consumes our early years. Our qualifications mark our arrival into the adult world. Our identity – if we are not careful – can become defined by what we do rather than who we are. Here we can lose ourselves if we fall into judging our worth according to our bank balance, car, holidays or designer brands. We can pull ourselves out of shape by using external measures and end up living – like Mr Duffy did in 'A Painful Case' the James Joyce *Dubliners* story – 'a short distance from our bodies'[3].

It might be an error to think that we need one big search, and all our questing is over. Rather in the trajectory of a long life or career we might need many mini searches to either research the new or remember what is important to us, so that we may recommit.

The words 'questing' and 'question' come from the same root in Latin. 'Searching' is all about listening to the silence when we can hear our souls speak. This type of searching is not a grasping, whereby we find *the* solution by sheer force of will, but rather a gentle invitation to step into the unknown – to go 'off-piste' – into both an unravelling and an unfolding. This can be a beautiful and sometimes a scary space where intuitions simply arrive – often obliquely – like silk threads. If we grab too forcefully, they will just break or disappear. The soul does not like to be rushed. Can we be patient enough?

Searching is daring to find our own path, to draw our own maps and to weave our own tapestries by following the wisdom of our hearts. In this way, we can come home to ourselves as we find our own place in the world – very personal fusions or never-ending conversations between our inner wild soul and our outer, more disparate roles.

Songlines

Invitation: What You are Seeking is Seeking You

Rumi wrote, 'What you are seeking is seeking you.'[4] So go for a walk in one of your favourite spots or walk a labyrinth and ask yourself, 'What is looking or wanting to find me?'. Walk slowly. Look for clues as you walk – but rather than forcing anything just be gently open to what arrives. Notice what you notice. Journal or take photos as you walk. When you are in a café or back home, journal what you've noticed. Make a commitment to repeat this practice until you recognize a settling within yourself. You can also do this practice at home in your sanctuary exploring your question as you journal, draw or craft.

A Journaling Practice

What is your invitation here? What needs to be searched and/or re-searched? What is calling you now – and what feels different from what went before?

Serendipity

'The world is full of magic things patiently waiting for our senses to grow sharper.'

W.B. Yeats[1]

Happy accidents invite us to allow in the sense that larger forces might be at play; sometimes we just have to get out of our own way.

Serendipity – or unplanned, happy accidents – can look and feel like magic. It can look like coincidence or synchronicity but is actually a radical act of asking beautiful questions and paying a refined attention to how life is moving through us and around us.

Serendipity is the art of conversation between our own inner and outer worlds, where the mysterious in the middle happens – a conversation (with ourselves or with others) which catches fine threads of as-yet-unformed connection, or new patterns which are also pregnant with possibility. Serendipity does not occur if we are dogged with the leaden weight of thinking we know the answers. It invites us to play in the shorelines and liminal spaces of possibility and to come to our questions

with open minds and loving hearts as we sink into our curiosity and not knowing. Serendipity happens when we let go of what we might be grasping or holding in clenched fists, in order to become children and beginners again.

Our rational minds have learnt to dismiss the notion of magic[2]. The favouring of the rational, the logical and the scientific over the magical and mystical has taught us to mistrust phenomena which we cannot directly observe or numerically quantify. This has also cut us off from enlisting or trusting our own intuition, and our inner wisdom. Here we discover that what we thought was the safety of dominion and control is not actually how life is or how it works — when we dare to loosen our straitjacket, we can step into other worlds.

These worlds are where we commune with our free child — with our imaginations, with our senses, with our souls and with nature. In these worlds, where instinct and intuition live, fresh connections are made, and the familiar turns unfamiliar, building or reshaping what already existed to become new. Here, we step into the vastness of infinity where we are only limited by our own imaginations. This is the magic of different threads coming together at a particular moment in time which cannot be replicated. What looks like spontaneity, synchronicity, coincidence or emergence is magic just waiting to be found.

Metaphor can be the bridge between these worlds. Find safe places where you can play, dream and dare to imagine. Not everything which bubbles up is feasible or practical — and even that which is, needs careful crafting — but being alive to serendipity enables us to refresh and drink from a different well in a generous and generative universe.

Songlines

Invitation: Opening Up to Possibility

One of the best ways to become open to serendipity is to hold our seriousness lightly and playfully – to get out of our own way. Do some loosening limbering up exercise like doodling with your non dominant hand, dancing to your favourite music or singing to your favourite song as you invite your playful inner child to step forward. Now look for the sparkle or magic in the everyday and ordinary as you pan out and think of the serendipity (or series of coincidences) which might have been in play when you first met your work or life partner, when you found your soul home, or the moment when your life suddenly took a different or unexpected turn for the better. Reflect back and sense into what was your inner state when you allowed yourself to lean into this serendipity, and how could you invite yourself to be more open to this as you move forward?

A Journaling Practice

Ask yourself, 'what role does magic and serendipity play in my life?' What preconditions make it possible? What happens as a result?

'The not-knowing is crucial to art, is what permits art to be made. Without the scanning process engendered by not-knowing, without the possibility of having the mind move in unanticipated directions, there would be no invention.'

Donald Barthelme[1]

We are designed to scan – but we must scan for opportunities as well as for threats.

We are hardwired to scan. During most of our waking hours we are scanning to make sense of our environment – to alert us to potential dangers or to help us to interpret and to make meaning of what we are experiencing.

It is interesting that the *Oxford English Dictionary* gives two opposing definitions of 'to scan' – to either look over or read quickly or to look at carefully, even forensically. Perhaps both apply – and the gift is in finding the balance between the two for each context we find ourselves in. Perhaps we are continually zooming out – scanning to check the landscape for anything unusual in some way before we then decide to zoom in – to

dive into the detail of something which has just literally caught our eye for curiosity or threat or the opportunity to make new connections.

Scanning is a survival mechanism, but it can also be a force for creativity as we notice new connections and patterns on the horizon for closer or close-up study. And so just as when we look through the aperture of a camera lens, we can only focus on either the horizon or the ground – on the background or the foreground but not properly both at the same time. Choices need to be made on what to focus in on and for how long in the present moment before something else changes.

We see things as we are. We all have filters and make assumptions about what we think we see which can block our direct experience of what we are actually seeing in the moment. Our filters – whether conscious or unconscious – determine what we allow in. Our filters can serve to protect us at times, but at others can force us into an anxious hypervigilance. Our filters can be created by our upbringing, the stories we tell ourselves and the ways that we might choose to find solace in the world, but once our brains look at the world in one way it is often difficult to see things from any other perspective. Filtering as we scan closes us down rather than opens us up to new insights and appreciations. Filtering excludes rather than includes. And, if we can dare to lift, widen, or deepen our filters we can dare to open ourselves up even more to the infinite variety and beauty in all of life.

And so, zooming out allows us to appreciate the bigger picture, the meta perspectives and the wider connections on the horizon and zooming in allows us to become intimate with the granularity of what is in on the ground in front of us. And we need both if we are to experience awe with all that we encounter.

Songlines

Practice: Zooming in and Zooming Out

Using a camera play with the aperture on the camera lens. Now focus on a scene. Zooming in and zooming out notice what you can see and what you choose to pay attention to both in the distance and close up, as well as what appears to the middle distance between the two. Journal about what you are drawn to and what you notice from the three different positions. If you get stuck in one of the three positions, reflect on how that might affect your ability to attend to the other perspectives. Now replay a conversation that you have had recently or in real time. Again, play with the three positions and notice what might be 'in' and what 'out' of your line of sight in each case – and reflect how this might affect your interpretations and your judgement.

A Journaling Practice

Reflect on your filters. What is getting in the way of you seeing clearly 'what is'? For example, this might be particular assumptions, prejudices or past experiences which – by default – are getting in the way of your present moment experience, where you are seeing things not as they are but as *you* are. Might you be too focused on one perspective or one interpretation – perhaps what is right in front of you – to see what lies behind? Might your filters force you to ask too much of yourself at times? List them. Journal on how your filters might be interfering with your ability to sensitively and appropriately scan or read a scene or a situation, as well as what is now being asked of you.

Symbols – and Sideways Thinking

'The soul never thinks without a picture.'

Aristotle[1]

Our imaginations speak to us in symbols and representations.

For William Blake and the Romantic poets our imagination was evidence of the Divine – of God (or Spirit) working through us. They believed that each of us has a divine spark within us – a longing which is waiting to be ignited by images, stories, nature, patterns, symbols and archetypes – and which could break through our everyday routines and respond to the yearnings of our human hearts, the sensations of our bodies and our souls' search for wholeness. Our early intuitive intimations often appear not with words but in pictures and symbols.

Our imaginations are what make us uniquely human. We know that artists, writers and creatives have always treasured this access to the mysteries

of their imaginal realm which nourishes and inspires them with images and symbols and speaks to them across time and space in ways which are both deeply personal and universal. This portal is open to all of us – if we choose to engage, to play and to listen.

When we find the courage to let go of what we think we know, our imagination allows images to speak, and insights to be received. This might be through archetypes and symbols which are held in the shared collective consciousness which speak to our shared human experience and which are available to help us to make meaning from our experiences[2]. Or it might be through images, symbols and metaphors which emerge from our own experience and are held in our own personal consciousness. Or it might be a blend of both, gathering up like a butterfly net that which is wanting to make itself known. And perhaps more than ever – when we are realizing that more of the same is no longer enough – we are being invited to find new ways to remember our primeval relationship to song, story, poetry, spell, magic, oracle, dreams, rituals and invocation as a source of inspiration and to unlock both ancient wisdom and create new knowing for ourselves. Our imaginations need our understanding, our appreciation, and our tender loving care as they show what else might be possible.

Often, our imaginations are best approached gently and obliquely, invited to play rather than be clumsily commanded into action. Intimations often arrive sideways, slanted and in oblique snatches when we least expect them. And this demands huge trust in our own creative process as we learn to wait and watch for these intonations to float like tiny bubbles to the surface because we are ready to receive them. And what if imagination and art are not frosting at all but the fountainhead of all human experience and human endeavour?

Songlines

Invitation: Planning Regular Artist's Dates

We need to build up our reservoirs of experiences and images so that we can feed our imaginations so that they, in turn, can feed us. Julia Cameron, author of *The Artist's Way*, talks of the danger of 'overfishing'[3] as she calls it, meaning that we have to feed our imaginations so they have a huge reservoir of images, memories, and experiences which we can call upon when we are called to create. The best way to do this is by organizing frequent Artist's Dates – to go to unfamiliar, out-of-the-way, or unusual places where we can feed our memory banks and nourish our imaginations. Here we are very deliberately and intentionally nurturing our symbolic life. We can trust that our impressions and experiences will mulch, ready to be drawn upon or reappear in unexpected ways.

A Journaling Practice

How do you imagine your imagination and the imaginal realm? How much time do you spend in your imagination? How do you create the conditions to feed your imagination? How do you dare to re-imagine?

Surprise

'Every block of stone has a statue inside it and it is the task of the sculptor to discover it.
I saw the angel in the marble and carved to set him free.'

Michelangelo[1]

Instructions for Life: Pay attention; Be surprised; Share.

Creativity is the art of delighting and of surprising ourselves – of making new connections where we can dare to stop what is no longer working, reshape the old or bring the new into being. Here we stand on the precipice of our not knowing and jump into the liminal space of the universe's mysterious soup and magical potential. Here the extraneous is stripped away and everything is pure and surprising possibility – a place where we can wonder, be astonished and be free to play[2].

Our creativity cannot be rushed or forced, and often arrives unbidden – welcomed for its apparent spontaneity and unpredictability when, in reality, it's the result of juices mulching away just out of our awareness. Creativity requires us to pay careful attention. She often emerges as a surprise –

appearing as a glorious inspiration, a blissful promise, an unexpressed potential or as an inconvenient truth waiting to be discovered.

Creativity invites us to courageously go beyond our egos and venture into undiscovered lands, to detach and let go of what we think we know, to allow ourselves to become vulnerable as we become explorers, artists, sculptors and tourists. Here we can dare to touch our poetic imaginations – escaping the prison of the everyday in order to see anew.

Our delight and surprise can often be the energy and the golden thread that pull us forward, gathering its own momentum as we play and explore what has emerged. This energy can resource us when the voices of our inner critic and editor would prefer to keep us small.

Nature reminds us that there is a seasonal necessity to let go to let come – a time for cutting back dead wood to enable new forests, flora and fauna to breathe and grow. Both creating and destroying need us to work with courage, kindness and grace. We need to honour life's creative flows and tensions within us without carelessly, selfishly or needlessly causing harm to others.

Creativity belongs to us all and returns us to our essence and source – and it is our beacon of hope in our fragmented, wonderful world. Creativity is our own personal dance with life, with nature and with all of creation. Creativity is our map towards connection and belonging both to ourselves and to the world. Our creativity is where our wild souls can come into contact with the luminous, the magical, the surprising, the mysterious and the spiritual. Creativity in this way is a spiritual practice because through our creativity we learn to find the freedom to give expression to our unique voice, our unique contribution, and our unique legacy in the world. Creativity requires us to surprise and to be surprised, to take risks, to show up and be seen. Creativity is the ultimate act of freedom. Creativity invites us to wake up, grow up, be alive and show up. And there is no one 'right' way. All ways are welcomed.

Songlines

Invitation: Opening to Surprise

Think back to a time when you were last surprised. What and where was the jolt felt in your body – and what did it feel like? What new or fresh perspective emerged for you when surprise arrived? Journal or draw your jolt and the story of your experience.

A Journaling Practice

Using the lines from Mary Oliver's poem 'A Bride Married to Amazement'[3] as inspiration free write for 5 minutes on what would happen if you were married to surprise and amazement – or if you committed to a daily practice of amazement. What might you sow, seed and sculpt as a result?

Simplicity

'Simplicity is the ultimate sophistication.'

Leonardo da Vinci[1]

Simplicity is the spaciousness that lies beyond confusion.

Our tendency can be to clutter or overload – to weigh down an idea or a relationship with too many layers, hiding behind them, thinking perhaps 'it' or 'we' are not enough. Or, unsure of our own truth, we can muffle our voice by using the voices of others. Extra material can also be used to conceal our own clumsiness, when we have rushed or not done our own thinking to arrive at the essence of a thing. At best this can confuse, and at its worst it can obscure – and our lack of clarity can be seen as a failure to be authentic or share something of ourselves with others.

Simplicity is stripping ourselves of the superficial, the distracting and the superfluous – so we can step through the eye of the needle[2]. Simplicity holds an essence and a purity that speaks to the heart. Sometimes we lose sight of the elegance and beauty of what simplicity can offer us. Simplicity says, '…stop!...', '…strip back…' or '…enough...'

So, inviting in simplicity is freeing. It is not empty or bare but full of lightness, potential and possibility. Simplification is an ongoing practice of remembering to clear our way – and get out of our own way – so that we can return to our essence. The quest for simplicity is a continual de-cluttering process.

Simplicity perhaps starts with the sentence 'I am enough' in the present moment. As opposed to taking ourselves away from our pure sense of 'enoughness' we risk self-sabotage with negative self-talk or critical perfectionist injunctions like 'but I need to know more', 'I need to have more', 'I forgot to', 'I need to do more', 'I need to affect something', or 'I should be elsewhere'[3].

Simplicity is sophisticated because it demands a level of dedicated attention, committed crafting and hard work to cut through – and move beyond – the layers of ambiguity, temptation and complexity to find what feels true and resonates inside and out. Sophistication is not defined by trendsetters or fashion houses, but is obtained is by paying attention with timeless wisdom and discernment.

Or perhaps the move to simplicity is prompted by a sense of our own impermanence and stripping back to what truly matters. Perhaps simplicity arrives with the realization of our own mortality. We will all die and so the only choice we have is how to live well.

Songlines

Invitation: Simplifying

Ground and centre yourself. Now choose a part of your life that fills very full, fast, overloaded, overwhelming and/or complicated. Sense into how this makes you feel. Now ask yourself what part of this you can either pause, stop or redesign. Start small with mini steps. Ask yourself 'Why, who or what does this serve?' or 'Do I still need this?' Notice your inner critic who wants to hold on, and reassure them that you have got this. Perhaps shred a document a day, rearrange a drawer, or donate some unused item to charity. Notice any relief or lightness in your body as you work – and remember to take a moment to congratulate yourself on the steps you have taken. Keep going, building on your micro steps until you feel a sense of momentum and progress.

A Journaling Practice

What is your radical and daring simplification or simplicity? How could you make simplifying and simplification an ongoing practice? How does it feel?

Silliness

'The human race has only one really effective weapon and that is laughter.'

Mark Twain[1]

Remember to smile – and perhaps lighten up a little.

We have learnt to be serious, careful, committed and earnest. As we grew up, being 'a good student' was prized as a hallmark of maturity. And there is much to be serious about in the trajectory of any human life, as we develop our own ethical codes to guide us, as we experience losses and bereavements, and as we awaken to the troubles of the world. And there is a time to be appropriately serious in a range of contexts – otherwise we cause offence, failing to meet others where they are.

Yet our seriousness can become a mask or habit that we can hide behind. It can stop us from risking ourselves, reaching out and touching the soul of another human being. We can find ourselves inhabiting the roles of Adult and Parent in Transactional Analysis terms and forget our inner messy and playful child[2]. Part of our being fully human is our ability to welcome all parts and all states of ourselves as well as our history in the present moment.

Inviting our inner child out to play tends to become a practice that we need to relearn in later life. Twisted out of shape by the demands of home and work, we 'serious' adults can lose our facility to play. As babies and young children, we discovered the world through our playful experimentation.

Only when we gift ourselves the time and space to have downtime, to get off the treadmill, to be light, to experiment, to giggle, to smile, to laugh out loud, to 'waste' time, to stop being a slave to productivity, to see the crazy and the ridiculous, to get things 'wrong' do we find our place of contribution and belonging. Only when we to allow ourselves to get curious and open to wonder do we remember what life really is. Here we can relax our vice-like grip on linear reality and start to see life in its kaleidoscopic – and often humorous – multicolours. In times of playfulness, we can find our flow. Playfulness feeds and nourishes our soul. Here we can dare to imagine and dream. Rather than being a luxury, this time is a necessity when we can find a refreshing freedom and meaning.

However, getting out of the way of our seriousness is not always easy or even enjoyable. This is because in seeking out our inner child, our inner critic (or critical parent) is activated, thinking that it serves us by keeping us safe in proscribed narrow boxes. Freedom can be anathema to our suited and booted selves. Perfectionism becomes the voice of our inner oppressor and editor. Perfectionism is the head ruling our warm heart and wild soul as they try to be free.

Songlines

Visualization: Finding our Inner Smile

Ground and centre yourself. As you settle, breathe into your heart. Think of something fun, joyous, silly or happy, or someone who always makes you smile or giggle. Breathe into that memory. Notice what changes in you and your body as you enjoy those moments. Now leave that memory and recentre. Next, think of something or someone who is serious and, again, notice what changes in you and your body. Now leave that memory as you recentre and return to perhaps the same or another memory which made you smile. Take a screenshot of that feeling if you can, remembering that your antidote to seriousness is just a breath away.

A Journaling Practice

What is your ratio of seriousness to playfulness? What is your relationship with seriousness and its antidote? What would you like to be remembered for – for example would you like to be remembered as a serious or a playful person? Or somewhere in between and what would this mean for you?

Souvenir

'Ever poised on that cusp between past and future, we tie memories to souvenirs like string to trees along life's path, marking the trail in case we lose ourselves around a bend of tomorrow's road.'

Susan Lendroth[1]

Souvenirs invite us to remember to remember – and sometimes to forget.

Our souvenirs help us to tell our story. They may be heirlooms which connect us to who and where we come from – while we also try to forge our own identity to be uniquely ourselves. Souvenirs can help us to remember to remember. They remind us where we have been – and what has mattered to us and what has shaped us. They can also prompt us to let go of them as we rewrite some parts of our stories from our past which might no longer be serving us, so that we can be fully present now. They can also remind us of our promises or invite us into new futures full of memories yet to be made.

In Greek mythology, Memory was understood to be the mother of the nine Muses – the nine forms of creative endeavour[2]. Our memories can

be represented in the souvenirs and mementos we keep – and the stories we bestow on our souvenirs. Our memories can be our golden thread giving us a bridge between what has gone, what is and what might be.

The definition of remembering in the *Oxford English Dictionary* is 'to keep in memory, not to forget, ... to know by heart'[3]. Remembering is also our own re-membering – bringing us back into wholeness. This attends to the lost, denied, neglected, dissociated, or cut-off parts which have been waiting in the shadows, ready to become reunited with us.

Our memories can inform, inspire and spice up our creativity, and it is through our re-membering that we can find our fullest creative selves.

Songlines

Invitation: Lost and Found

Ground and centre yourself. Perhaps everything we have is a souvenir of a time and place we were once in? For this practice, bring your awareness to the room or, if you are outside, the area you find yourself standing in. With a soft focus look around you. Alight upon the picture or object that attracts your eye. Try to think back to the time you got it or were given it. Where were you? Who were you with? What memories or feelings does it evoke and what story does it hold for you? If you can, make the object feel like a part of you and as you do, ponder what its message from the past is here for you in the present and for your future. Journal or draw what you notice.

A Journaling Practice

Who is the 'you' who is witnessing your memories and also your forgettings? What memories – lost, re-found or refreshed – might need to be recalled in service of your fullest creative expression? What journey of re-membering might be needed for you to find a fuller embodied sense of your wholeness?

Rest and Return

'I am arriving
I am home
I am home
I am arriving.'

Thich Nhat Hanh, Plum Village Song

1. Strolling
2. Spirit as Love in Action
3. Skills for Life
4. Study
5. Stitching
6. Structure
7. Strength as Courage
8. Service
9. Society
10. Stewardship
11. Sharing
12. Sorry
13. Support
14. Sleep
15. Self-Care
16. Solace
17. So

Strolling

'Perhaps the truth depends on a walk around the lake.'

Wallace Stevens[1]

Strolling enables us to connect with our natural rhythms – as well as with those of nature.

Walking frees us to think without wallowing in our thoughts. Stimulated and supported by what our senses take in, our minds can flit through time, hovering from observations to memories to dreams and to action. This often helps settle previously jumbled thoughts and ideas. We can – if we allow ourselves to – feel held by the rhythms of our feet and our breath. Nature's generosity can fire our imagination as we appreciate the bigger picture. On foot everything comes into connection. Walking labyrinths or pilgrimages can bring us back ourselves while they lead us to their centre or destination. The road – our road – is made by walking.

Strolling is an invitation to join with nature. It gives us freedom, choice and independence. Our bodies were made for movement. Walking slows us. It is universal, egalitarian and democratic. Nobody teaches us to walk – as toddlers we just play, stumble and find our way.

In our strolling we discover the joy of uncluttered time. We find a settling into silence and solitude. We open up to awe. We become enchanted and our hearts and minds start to wander and wonder. When we give ourselves to places, these places give back to us. Getting lost as we walk is often as important as finding ourselves. In our lostness we allow life to find us. Here we are reminded that we are only made to focus on one thing at a time – either on the horizon or the ground.

The English language is full of walking allusions and metaphors, which shows it is more than just a way of getting from A to B: 'one step at a time', 'tread carefully', 'there's a mountain to climb'.

Perhaps you could learn to be more of a Flâneur. This is a French term used by the 19th-century French poet Charles Baudelaire, meaning 'stroller' or 'loafer'. A Flâneur strolls through their days, wandering and wondering and occasionally pausing to admire the sights.

Songlines

Practice: Step by Step

When you are next out walking, take time to really feel your feet on the ground. Perhaps even walk barefooted. Focus either on the ground or the horizon and explore the different perspectives this brings. Observe yourself as you walk, noticing how the rhythms of walking start to settle your mind and your body, giving you luxurious time and space for your thoughts to wander.

A Journaling Practice

How do you use strolling or walking to support yourself and your work? How might you slow down to become a Flâneur in your own life? How might you elevate strolling into a new art form for yourself and your work?

Spirit as Love in Action

'Only love expands intelligence. To live in love is to accept the other and the conditions of this existence as a source of richness, not as opposition, restriction, or limitation.'

Humberto Maturana[1]

What if we were to awaken and open our hearts to give and receive love?

Spirit breaths air and life into us. Spirit animates. Spirit is a particular way of thinking, feeling, and behaving within a group or a community. And so, what becomes possible if we are able to see the source – or the organizing principle of the universe – as love and the natural state of the universe as one of respectful loving connection? What if our own spiritual journey is the work of awakening and opening our hearts to give and receive love in all its forms and guises?[2.] Knowing that we can return to our own source of love gives us hope and helps us to build resilience. What becomes possible when we are powered by love?

Love here is defined not only as romantic love but by an ongoing unconditional acceptance of ourselves and of others with all of our glorious gifts, brilliance, vulnerabilities, clumsiness and stuckness.

Love in this way can be seen as the source of pure energy which changes matter. Love elevates and transcends. Love is infinite, renewing and renewable. Love is not blind but wise, intelligent and savvy. Love needs to be claimed to become the language and lens of all endeavours – and not some embarrassed fumbled word reserved for our non-work activities.

When we live and create from this source, we are in effect channelling the universal force of love – be it love for our ourselves, for another, for our families, for our friends, for our projects or for our world. This gives our being or our body of work a unique, pure and authentic voice, which is ours alone to own and which others can recognize and resonate with, because it comes from our love – the Source – of our being. When we die, we are remembered more for what and how we loved than for our career progression.

Love comes naturally. Fear is what we learn. To learn to love ourselves as we learn to love (or unconditionally accept) others is a lifetime's spiritual journey – with all the possible heartbreaks along the way – where we can often stumble, fail and falter but where even in the act of our very trying, we can learn and grow. And what becomes possible – how might we dare or risk ourselves – if we carry the knowledge that our hearts are big enough to hold everything without breaking? For Rumi our task is not to seek love but to simply remove all the barriers that we have built against it[3]. The pain we feel is a measure of the depth and sincerity of our engagement with life – our attempts to shape a more mature, loving, spacious, compassionate and generous version of ourselves. And this love can also be 'tough love' when honesty is needed from ourselves and others to help us to stay on track.

And yet love needs hospitable and generous conditions to thrive. We know love as a presence which we can experience as connecting, inspiring, supporting, encouraging and resourcing us, enabling us to thrive and flourish. We can also know of its absence, where disconnection, contraction, judgement, harshness and coldness are experienced. When we live and work from a place of love, we can be generous, hospitable, kind and forgiving.

Songlines

Invitation: A Deep Time Meditation

Find a timeline which charts the evolution of Earth, and reflect upon it, memorizing a few of the key dates if that works for you. See www.earthow.com or www.deeptimewalk.org for a chart. Now ground and centre yourself and as you breathe, take a walk through time – as far as your imagination can go – to the source of everything. Ask yourself how respect – if not love – has played out in our evolution? When you leave your meditation, journal what you have noticed and the questions which may have surfaced for you.

A Journaling Practice

How might love infuse your practice? Instead of reacting to a challenging situation, dare you ask yourself, 'What is the most loving thought, feeling or action I can make or extend right now in this moment?' Journal what you notice.

Skills for Life

'Know all the theories, master all the techniques, but as you touch a human soul be just another human soul.'

C.G. Jung[1]

The talents we really need might not be the ones we think.

Skills and competence are necessary for entering any trade or profession. Theories, processes and techniques are important tools for the toolbox and necessary for our Certifications and Accreditations. But these are just maps and not the territory.

Our highly prized techniques and tools are important but can never be enough. In our human work we need to get beyond them to be with other human beings. We are not machines applying formulae. For those of us who are leaders or people professionals we need to learn how to put down our masks, rest our – often expensively acquired – certificates and qualifications and travel from our heads to our hearts to do the human work, which is love. Love here is not romantic love but the unconditional acceptance of ourselves and others.

In order to earn the privilege and honour of working with another human being, we must first embrace our *own* humanness. This also invites us to own all our strengths, vulnerabilities and shadows. Then we have a chance to find the spaciousness and courage to be compassionate wise witnesses to the experience of others. Because it is only when we own our vulnerabilities – our uncertainties, our anxieties, our attachments – that the potential for true learning and growth emerges[2]. Being with this not knowing, being easeful and graceful in unformed uncertainty, being patient and trusting with how emergence works, opens new portals to possibility.

The good news is that we already have the heart-based, love-filled qualities necessary to bring our work alive in this way, because we are born with them.

Songlines

Meditation: The Task of the Craftsperson

Ground and centre yourself as you reflect on how you might become a beginner again in some aspect of your life and work. As you reflect, notice your attachments, conditioning and what might be holding you back from bringing fresh eyes and a beginner's mindset to this. Play with the image of the sculptor as you bring the pure intention of discovering the essence and shape of what lies beneath. Notice what shifts and what frees in you as you explore. Journal what you notice. You might also want to read 'The Woodcarver' by Chuang Tzu which speaks of the beauty that can be created once the inner work is done[3].

A Journaling Practice

What are the human qualities which you would like to make more alive in your life or work? What new ones would you like to invite into your work? What familiar ones would you like to nurture? What does working with a beginner's mindset mean for you — and how might you be able to begin again and again with each new encounter?

Study

'There are two kinds of intelligence: one acquired,
as a child in school memorizes facts and concepts
from books and from what the teacher says,
collecting information from the traditional sciences
as well as from the new sciences.
With such intelligence you rise in the world.

There is another kind of tablet, one
already completed and preserved inside you.
A spring overflowing its springbox. A freshness
in the centre of the chest. This other intelligence
does not turn yellow or stagnate. It's fluid,
and it doesn't move from outside to inside
through conduits of plumbing-learning.
This second knowing is a fountainhead
from within you, moving out.'
Rumi[1]

Learning should keep us free.

Too often, studying has become associated with the grind of schoolwork, qualifications, and accreditations. Here there is pressure to study the given curriculum well, in order to make our way in the world. And it is here that the harsh memories of often tortuous shifting processes – where we were judged on our academic prowess and our scoreboard of grades – stay lodged in our psyche, undermining our confidence and keeping us small. In this harsh environment, the joy of learning can be overlooked – if not completely forgotten. The result is that many of us therefore exit our educational systems exhausted and having fallen out of love with learning. And yet our capacity for deep reflective learning is one of the only true forms of durable capital we own.

So, what happens – and what becomes possible – if we can reframe study as joyful intimate discovery of new vistas where we follow our curiosity and what we love? What if we come to see the study of ourselves, others and our world as an infinite road of endless fascination, wonder, learning and creativity? What happens if we tap into our innate human need to develop, to adapt and to learn, relearn and unlearn? What if we came to understand that reflection – a key and often overlooked facet of the learning process – is an inexhaustible, ever-present, innate capacity we all have, to adapt, thrive and live well? And what happens if we can all convince ourselves that we are not broken but are exploring our learning edges?[2] It is only when we drop our masks and make ourselves vulnerable in our not knowing that we can learn. In our studies and studying we sit at the feet of our experience – and only we can know what that experience is. Our responsibility is to make sense of that experience before we can make meaning from it. But the deal is that with this vulnerability we also need to give ourselves huge doses of compassion as we stumble to keep ourselves engaged and resilient.

Like artists or dancers, we need to understand that studying the classic fundamentals of any field is only the entry point to that craft, sphere, or profession. As we grow into our chosen area, we should continue to acquire more technical knowledge, but this must not overshadow the journey we make into ourselves. Reflective learning enables self-authoring and self-referencing so that we can make meaning from our own experiences – and not from what we are taught or absorb from others. Stepping away from the need to be 'right' and the judging of 'wrong' means that we can meet soul-to-soul and heart-to-heart in the universal field of generative learning and potential[3].

Songlines

Visualization: Learning from Love (not Fear)

Tap into some of your learning experiences. How do you like to learn when you feel free? What was a good learning experience for you? Why was it so? Now think of a less than good learning experience for you – and again notice how it makes you feel. Now return to another good learning experience for you – and again notice how it made you feel. Then start to zoom out and notice the preconditions you need to support you and your learning from love (and not fear or a feeling of not being enough) and choose how you would like to bring more of these preconditions into your life

A Journaling Practice

Ask yourself what your relationship with study is from the past, in the present and what might you like it to be in the future? What is your preferred style – are your pragmatist, an activist, a theorist, or a reflector? Or a combination of all four? And how might this be changing as you mature?

Stitching

'We stitch together quilts of meaning to keep us warm and safe, with whatever patches of beauty and utility we have on hand.'

Anne Lamont[1]

We create our lives as we sew or weave, stitch by stitch.

Making a life is like sewing a patchwork quilt – and we are the stitcher and master storyteller. Each quilt tells a story which is entirely our own. The fabric of our lives is made up of many different – often random – patches of cloth which we gather up as we walk through life – sewn together with love and care to create something which is both beautiful and useful. The whole quilt is so much more important than any single piece.

As we proceed, we can be putting together our own designs. We can choose many different fabrics which can be of many colours, hues and textures to tell our stories. And as we sew, we need to decide which patches go side by side, which need to be kept apart or even discarded? What colour thread should be used to stitch the pieces together – should the thread blend, stand out or be invisible? Where might we want to

decorate and embroider, adding new layers of materials, texture and meaning? And where do holes, tears or dropped stitches need to be left because they let the light in? Or might they need repairing? What form might the borders or boundaries take?

Sewing is also a practical craft which anybody can do – and we create, one stitch at a time. It is also a meditative practice and for many can also be a healing practice – calming and soothing because of the repetition required. As we sew, we can tune into our own thoughts, feelings, and hopes for the future. In our sewing we take one step at a time and only when we stop and reflect do we see the bigger patterns emerging mirrored back to ourselves. What old patterns or habits are still holding us hostage and what new patterns are wanting to emerge and make themselves known to us? What do we want to refresh or upcycle with the rags we already have and what new designs do we want to create?

Stitched into the patchwork of our lives is the golden thread of who we are. Our golden thread is our birth right, helping us to remain true to our soul's own unique code. It is that part of ourselves which is present in everything, stitching together all the disparate stories and parts of ourselves to pattern – and celebrate – the whole.

Songlines

Practice: Finding your Golden Thread!

Take a plain piece of A4 paper. Turn your page lengthways (or in landscape mode). Now write across your page listing all the things which have resourced or sustained you up to now. Here is the warp of your life – the warp is the ground of your life and are those things which hold you in place. Now turn your page sideways (or in portrait mode). Now write across the page writing all the qualities you need or heart requests you want to make to keep going. Here is the weft of your life — your own hopes and dreams. And then taking an overview of all that you have written circle in a different colour your standout words and draw a dark line between them. This is your golden thread[2].

A Journaling Practice

On a large piece of paper draw eight squares. Decide on a question or an issue you want to explore. Take your coloured pens, crayons or paints and create a pattern in each square which represents an aspect of your question. If needed, make notes in the margin as you go. Continue until all 8 squares are coloured in. Now take a bright colour as your golden thread and link the squares together in new and different ways. Journal on what emerged for you as

Structure

'We are what we repeatedly do. Excellence, then, is not an act, but a habit.'

Will Durant[1]

Structures hold us and keep us in a shape.

Structure – and having a structure – gives us a home base from which we can contribute to the world. Having a structure gives us some basic organizing shape and design principles into which we can give ourselves permission to muse, to dream or to work.

Structures provide frameworks and boundaries – ways of diarizing and theming our days and our weeks – which can give meaning and purpose because how we spend our moments is how we end up spending our lives. Children like both structure and free play for their imaginations to wander. And as with children so with us: too much structure leads to constriction and too much unstructured space leads to self-indulgence and chaos. Less structure is needed when things need to emerge; and more structure is needed when we shift from the unknown to the known to craft whatever action is needed. We need to find the balance for ourselves which also honours our own energies, our passions and the different contexts that we are in.

And structures do not need to be corsets, draining our lifeblood but rather give us a shape which can free our creativity, knowing also that everything will also get done when the time is right. Structures also should not be confused with routine and its punitive or deadening undertones but seen as gentle rituals where we intentionally mark the transition — our crossing the threshold — from one activity to the next. This could be as simple as lighting a candle or taking a deep breath to signal to shift from one context to another. Routines are what we might mindlessly allow ourselves to fall into whereas having a structure and a discipline is what we dedicate ourselves to. What we intend — and what we hope for — shapes the structures we design around ourselves.

Structures — which could be seen as a gentle ritualizing of our day — hold us accountable without the guilt because we have already contracted with ourselves what needs our focus at a particular time. Having a structure gives us a pattern to our days — where there is some consistency and predictability and where our brains can be made ready — primed for the work before the work.

So often we push and force against our own natural rhythms which leads to frustration and disappointment in what we ultimately produce. Having a structure enables us to match the task with the energy it requires — for example many writers prefer to write in the morning because that is when they feel most creative and leave their more administrative duties to the afternoon. And so, perhaps seeing each part of the day as having its own season might help us to better honour our own rhythms — for example of seeing of spring in the morning as a time of creativity, of summer at lunchtime with a blossoming of the work, of late summer after lunch with a savouring and conservation, of autumn in the late afternoon as a time of pruning and clarifying and of winter in the evening as a time of rest and retreat, as well as readying ourselves for the next day. Gentle structures support our wellbeing and self-esteem as they also help us to be honest with our expectations of ourselves – to be clear with ourselves and with others what is achievable and what is not within a set period of time.

Songlines

Visualization: Seeing Your Diary as a Palette

Draw an artist's palette. Now draw up a list of the main themes and activities which make up your life – and then match the energy and focus that these require of you. Group them and then see how you might be able to better structure your days and week. You might even want to allocate green activities for the springtime of your day; red activities for the summertime of your day; orange activities for the late summertime of your day; grey activities for the autumn of your day; and blue activities for the wintertime of your day.

A Journaling Practice

Ask yourself 'What is my relationship to structure?' and 'Where do I have too much or too little structure and what are the consequences of this for me?'

Strength as Courage

'Being deeply loved by someone gives you strength, while loving someone deeply gives you courage.'

Lao Tzu[1]

Strength is an intelligent suppleness of the heart.

We have a culture of prizing strength and being seen as strong – of continuing despite the odds through sheer force of will. And yes, there is a place for this, but pure strength can be overplayed when it is not wrapped up in the wisdom of the heart. What might be possible if we wrapped strength in tender, heart-based courage?

A courageous strength enables us to embrace our vulnerabilities and see them as our own unique lens on the world – the seat of our own humanity and the seat of our shared connection with others. Here we can reframe our vulnerabilities and see them not as weaknesses but as vital qualities which keep us alive and awake enabling us to be with the unknown, which is also the birthplace of our connection and creativity.

This strength enables us to drop our straitjackets and learn to accept life's messiness and muddle with an enabling equanimity. And when we work with 'what is' rather than fighting 'what if' we are able to step into our resilience to reshape, reframe or create anew.

And is often experienced as a quiet inward manoeuvre – the inward preparation of our interior landscape to shape how we show up in the work. This is how we can choose to take our place, to hold our ground, and to have our voice heard whilst deeply respecting the right of others to do the same.

This wise strength is also the ability to keep going even when we don't want to – but is not endurance for endurance's sake and we need to develop the wisdom to know when it is necessary and appropriate for us to pause or to stop. And our strength also paradoxically knows when we need to ask for help. Courage is not always comfortable, but it helps us to get up and dust ourselves off, in spite of setbacks, make errors and learn from them, and to continue to be curious, to experiment, to laugh at ourselves and to stay in love with life. From here we can find the grounded equanimity to find the spaces between fear and compassion where loving kindness to ourselves and to others can flourish.

Strength is also the road to equanimity – the courage and the willingness to accept things (whatever they are) as they are, in this moment. Equanimity brings calmness and balance to moments of joy as well as difficulty. Equanimity is like the calm eye in the centre of the storm – which grounds us in the knowledge that everything is constantly changing and much of it is out of our control. 'Upekkha' is a compound word in the ancient Buddhist language of Pali.[2] It can be translated as 'calmly observing' or 'viewing with patience and wisdom'. This courage and equanimity help us find our own route through our fear, overwhelm, impatience, reluctance and judgement to a remembering of love, compassion and connection.

Songlines

Visualization: Being the Willow Tree

Find a photograph of a willow tree – or if you have one close by go and stand under it. Willow trees are large trees with long, flowing branches and leaves, often used to symbolize flexibility and adaptability. The limber and supple nature of its extremities means it bends to accommodate and withstand strong winds and adverse weather. **And** so ground and centre yourself as you feel yourself settle and start to absorb with the qualities of the willow tree. Breathe in its strength, its flexibility, its adaptability, its resilience and its grace. Start to merge with the tree, and as you do so ask yourself 'How could I become more like the willow tree?' When you are ready, come out of the visualization and journal what has arisen in you.

A Journaling Practice

What stories do you tell yourself about strength and being strong? How are they serving you? What would happen if you wrapped strength in a blanket of courage – and what then would courage look like for you?

Service

'Work is love made visible. And if you cannot work with love but only with distaste, it is better that you should leave your work and sit at the gate of the temple and take alms of those who work with joy.'

Kahlil Gibran[1]

Service is love in action.

Service is work with love. Work is the place where our soul and our role can have the opportunity to meet and dance in unison and be made visible in the world.

All our best work comes from the heart. Falling in love – and staying in love – with our work is the challenge of any long professional life. All 'people work' is at its essence heart work. Without love – love of the work or the love of families and/or hobbies which the work supports – work can feel soulless. And how many people can love what they do and do what they love? What is needed to find the love of work and then to keep our love fresh and alive?

The seed of our purpose is often to found in our own stories and what we have learnt from there. What we know most deeply and what we have learnt most about, is our offer to the world. 'Samu' (作務) is defined by the Zen tradition as 'work practice' where we put what we have learnt into service without delay. This term emerged from the monks who insisted that monastic communities should be self-supporting and not reliant on donations from lay benefactors.

Our work is actually an intimacy written large, since it is the place where we (the self) meet the world. Work – in all its forms – is where we find our belonging in the world. The empowering invitation here is to dare to reframe our definitions of outward recognition, wealth or success. Our work stays alive by our willingness to open ourselves up to all the frustrations, heartbreaks and difficulties – as well as the joys and exhilarations – of our being in service of something bigger or beyond ourselves.

Work that comes from the central conversation within ourselves of 'Who am I?' and 'What is my work?' embodies an authenticity, a freshness and a vibrancy which is immediately recognizable. We feel most truly alive when we are in alignment – when we dare to be the song that our heart wants to sing. It is this song that people around us respond to.

Songlines

Inquiry: 'What Does Being in Service Mean?'

This is a walking meditation and reflection. As you step outside, ask yourself how you feel about being 'a servant' and the baggage you might hold or have absorbed around that term. Ask yourself what other interpretations might be possible for you. Then ask yourself, 'What is the role of a servant?' and start to ponder where in your life you might be working or have worked in the genuine service of another. Then think about those places where your own ego, agenda, will or mastery might have got in the way. What did that feel like for you? Ask yourself what might be needed from you to see work as service and as love in action.

A Journaling Practice

Do you love what you do? What is needed to keep your love for your work fresh and alive? Is work a job, a vocation, or a spiritual practice for you? How can you serve without losing or sacrificing yourself? Is your role work an expression of your soul's whisperings?

Society

'When we originally went to the Moon, our total focus was on the Moon. We weren't thinking about looking back at the Earth. But now that we've done it, that may well have been the most important reason we went.'

David Beaver, co-founder of the Overview Institute[1]

The meaning of life is found in our relationships.

The human world is made up of an interconnected web of relationships – and relationships are built one conversation at a time. Finding our proper place depends on being curious and accepting people who are not us – which is everyone. Because as Thich Nhat Hanh writes 'we inter-are'[2].

'Society' or 'a society' is a community or group of people having common traditions, institutions and interests which also depend on the tolerance and acceptance of other societies to survive and to thrive[3].

A sense of place and belonging is a basic human need. And perhaps we are all looking for our own 'society' or 'tribe' – a collection of people which we can call home, where we feel seen, welcome and where we feel we belong. This can be easy for some but can be a lifelong quest for others.

Homecomings

We are hardwired to notice who or what is unfamiliar or different but how we hold our noticing – and what we 'do' with our noticing – is what matters when it comes to living with ease, elegance and grace. The work of Black Lives Matter and the LGBTQ+ community to name just two, highlights the danger and damage that can be inflicted on individual lives as well as whole societies when we discriminate, exclude and/or persecute.

In 1968, the Apollo 8 astronauts felt overwhelmed by the beauty, unity, fragility and vulnerability of Earth suspended in the void of the cosmos. From space, there are no borders, countries or boundaries, just one earth and one people.

When we come to an embodied appreciation of our own interconnectedness with all of life, we are forever changed. We find ourselves experiencing new levels of awe, intimacy and reverence for life. It does not matter what our starting or entry point is, but as we open ourselves up to how life works holistically, a shift in consciousness occurs in us, which is compassionate, humane and respectful. This shift can become a new lodestar infusing our ways of being, relating and doing.

What if we were to organize into 'sanghas' or spiritual communities? 'Sangha' comes from Buddhism and means 'association' or 'society' but in its broadest sense it is the ideal of a spiritual friendship group – a fellowship of support with those who are broadly on the same path towards Enlightenment. This is a sangha of soul friends practicing together to bring about and maintain awareness[3]. Its purpose is to foster love, harmony, awareness, acceptance and understanding. When we dare to take our learning and questions into 'sanghas' of fellow travellers and like-minded souls, we can hold up a mirror to ourselves – as we gently hold the mirror up to others – to examine who we are, how we work and what needs our attention.

Songlines

Inquiry: Becoming More Sangha-like

This is a reflective inquiry and visualization. This practice asks, 'How might the spirit of sangha – in either secular or religious forms depending on your own context – be created and expressed in your life and work?'; 'How can we create different forms of sangha so that we can see ourselves as fellow travellers, seeking companionship, inspiration, challenge and support in a shared quest for greater and greater insight, awareness, self-knowledge and learning?'; 'How can we find our tribe of fellow travellers?'; 'What contracting is needed to bring the spirit of sangha alive in your life or work?'; and 'When we do not see the essence of sangha in our life and work how can you name this?'

A Journaling Practice

What does home, place and belonging look and feel like for you? What does 'society' mean for you? Have you found your tribe or tribes? How do you 'other' what is not you? How do you welcome, respect and work with difference, diversity and inclusion?

Stewardship

'Our task is to gather the treasures of the past into the competencies of the present for the wellbeing of the future.'

Maori Proverb

Without stewardship in a community, nothing can be truly cared for.

A steward is someone who cares for and looks after people and resources for an allotted time. A steward feels a sense of history and the preciousness of life. They feel responsible for honouring the treasures and legacy of the past, whilst at the same time using present resources in service for the sustainable wellbeing of all of life both now and in the future.

Stewardship is not a fashionable term but it is an important one that also keeps us humble. It reminds us that we are born with nothing and will die with nothing and that in this life (or reincarnation) we are just passing through. Good stewardship applies as much to ourselves as to our wider familial and societal responsibilities.

How we treat our precious earth holds a mirror up to how we also treat ourselves. Many of us are run by scripts of 'do more' and 'do it faster'. The impact of humanity's overconsumption and exploitation of the earth's resources is being felt in almost every corner of the globe where changes in local weather systems are being reported with drastic effects for our biodiversity, water tables and soil health. And as with the earth, we forget to attend to our own self-care – the stewardship of ourselves. Taking care – and respecting other sentient and non-sentient beings – starts at home.

Stewards are generous legacy makers. They see their actions across time and within the wider arc of the cycle of life. The protection of what is worth preserving and conserving is their priority – and to leave the world in a little bit of a better shape because of their own particular version of caring. To establish what this is for each of us, the practice of stewardship might start with the heartfelt appreciation of what we truly treasure and marvel at – and without which the world would be a less beautiful or a more diminished place.

With this perspective, can we hear the voices both of our ancestors and of future generations, calling to us and guiding us? What kind of stewardship do they need from us at this time? Can each of us become a loving steward in our communities and a mindful caretaker of the land and the resources we use? Perhaps we can step into our own wise elderhood and work with nature's checks and balances to ensure that what we already have can be sustained? Perhaps we can find eco alternatives so that what we take can be replaced?

Songlines

Practice: Defining your own Stewardship

Find your watercolour paints and paper together with some sharpies or felt tip pens. Paint a background of different colours onto your paper. Allow this to dry. When it is dry draw a big heart in the centre, and then draw a second line around it leaving enough space to write between the lines. Now think of the qualities that you would like to bring to your stewardship and write these between the lines. When you have done this divide the inside of the heart into 4 to 6 sections. Write into each section what actions or projects you will undertake to bring your stewardship alive. You have now made a manifesto or statement of your stewardship, and how you will embody it. Consider how you might want to share this with others – or invite others to do the same.

A Journaling Practice

Write a short paragraph or poem which explores what stewardship means for you – as well as how you might like to cultivate your caring to what is important to you going forward in your life and work.

Sharing

'There is no joy in possession without sharing.'

Erasmus[1]

How we share shows others how we care.

Indigenous wisdom knows the value of the gift economy. In a gift economy, goods and services are exchanged between people within a community without expectation of a direct payment or trade being made in return. This enables the sharing and free flow of skill, expertise, materials or food between the earth and people (and between each other) based on pure need rather than want or desire.

Sharing is based on the practices of mutuality, co-operation and exchange. It can also be an act of fair exchange – a mutual giving and taking – or an act of redistribution to fill gaps, meeting needs from places of relative abundance and plenty. Sharing honours the cycle of life for all living things and helps to remind us that we belong.

Homecomings

When we can appreciate everything as a 'gift' originating in some way from the world's natural resources – and not as 'commodities' or 'products' to be consumed – our relationship with it also changes. We stop taking it for granted. Perhaps we can see ourselves become more humble as we start to explore our place in the chain of life. A gift economy based on giving and passing on the surplus, nurtures the bonds of community which, in turn, enhances the mutual wellbeing and flourishing of all.

Robin Wall Kimmerer writes about the lessons we can learn from the concept of 'The Honourable Harvest'[2]. The 'Honourable Harvest' is a term which embodies the traditional ideas about the exchange of life for life. The rules are not formally written down but if they were they would look something like this:

- Know the ways of the ones who care for us – the plants which are our food and medicine – so that we, in turn, can take care of them.
- Ask permission before taking and abide by the answer.
- Never take first or last and only take what you need.
- Take only what is yours.
- Never take more than half and leave some for others.
- Use what you have respectfully, share and never waste what you have taken.
- Give thanks for what you have been given and give a gift of reciprocity for what you have been given.

When we were young, we were taught the importance of sharing, but we risk losing sight of these lessons as we try to forge our own identities and gain our status symbols of job, home, car and consumables. But what is enough? We are inhospitable guests on planet earth, consuming more than earth can sustain. Sharing what we already have through gifting, reuse, repurposing, or recycling is not just a personal matter but a political and planetary necessity. At the core of both country and world geopolitics is the fundamental question of how people can (or cannot) more equally share what is available – to find a fairer means of distribution between the 'haves' and the 'have nots'.

Songlines

Invitation: Practices for More Intentional Sharing

Choose a room in your house. Review what is in this space that you could better share, repurpose, or recycle in some way and take appropriate action accordingly. Then repeat choosing another area. Or start a Gratitude Practice Balance Sheet. In your journal, divide the paper into two lengthways. In the left-hand column write Gratitude Practice and in the right-hand column write Reciprocal Practice. At the end of each day write what you are grateful for and how you may reciprocate in big or small ways.

A Journaling Practice

Take the principles of the Honourable Harvest above and apply to some aspect of your work or home life. Then write about how you currently live into these in this area – even scoring yourself on a score of 0 to 10 where 0 is not at all and 10 is all the time. Next, write what you would like to change. Return to your journal entry in a month's time and review what feels different. Repeat the practice.

Sorry

'An apology is a lovely perfume; it can transform the clumsiest moment into a gracious gift.'

Margaret Lee Runbeck[1]

Saying sorry can be an act of kindness to ourselves – and often unsticks both the giver and the receiver.

The word 'sorry' is a small but perhaps underused word in the English language.

Our fragile egos like us to be right or perfect. Saying 'sorry' is the discipline of getting beyond this, to put ourselves in the other person's shoes. Saying 'sorry' is a practice of building bridges where we try to meet each other beyond the fields of right or wrong.

We need lovingly to accept that we all make mistakes or errors of judgement – that in our rush we might not read a situation well and can be blind to the delicacies or sensitivities of the other. So, saying 'sorry' – and really meaning it – is first an act of compassion and kindness to ourselves. We are accepting that we are not perfect and that what we intended was not what was experienced by the other. In accepting that we did cause upset, distress or offence by our words or actions, we can start to make good our error. Saying 'sorry' honours the other and is a mature act of accepting personal responsibility when things go wrong, as well as opening up the possibility of reparation.

In our accepting a 'sorry' from another is our own internal move to get beyond the hurt into the future through forgiveness. When we close down by refusing to say 'sorry' or refusing to accept an apology, this can diminish both parties. History is littered with tales of slights received and grievances powerfully held which create disruptions and fractures, sometimes for a while and sometimes for lifetimes or across generations.

Saying 'sorry' and receiving a 'sorry' takes us into the field of our shared humanity. It might be that the part of us which is hurt can never forgive. However, it might also be true that our forgiveness rarely comes from the part of us that was wounded but is transcended by the heathier or stronger parts of ourselves. This makes forgiveness an act of connection and compassion coming from the healthy rather than wounded part of ourselves – which is not therefore a passive act of simply forgetting or ignoring. Forgiveness invites us into a larger identity and reminds us that we can all fumble, stumble and fall.

Kintsugi, also known as 'kintsukuroi', is the Japanese art of repairing broken pottery by mending the areas of breakage with lacquer dusted or mixed with powdered gold, silver or platinum – and so broken pottery is repaired but is also made stronger and more beautiful than its original state. The promise and the invitation of kintsugi infuses every apology which is ever made or received. And perhaps our errors can be reframed as threshold invitations to step into a deeper understanding, connection and respect for the other.

Songlines

Reflective Walk: Is 'Sorry' the Hardest Word?

Make some time to consider your relationship with being sorry. Think back to when someone tried to apologize to you, and you did not hear it or receive it. What happened? How did you feel? What can you learn from this? Now think back to a time when you said sorry to another person. What happened? How did you feel? What can you learn from this? When have you refused to say sorry – or said sorry and not meant it? Think about times when saying sorry was both overplayed and underplayed. What made it so? Journal or draw your reflections.

A Journaling Practice

What is your relationship with the word 'sorry' and saying 'sorry'? What is your relationship to forgiving and also to being forgiven?

Support

'Life is not a solo act. It's a huge collaboration, and we all need to assemble around us the people who care about us and support us in times of strife.'

Tim Gunn

Asking for support can be one of the bravest things we can do.

Why we care, who we care for and how we care define us. Do we care and support from a mature, responsible stance, which seeks to enable rather than patronize or diminish? To paraphrase Theodore Roosevelt: 'Nobody cares how much you know, until they know how much you care.'

And our care and support are often expressed not in grand statements or big dictates but in small thoughtful acts. Support is not something to be imposed on another but offered through sensing and reading another and their context. It is given and received through a dance of reciprocity and mutuality which empowers both rather than reducing them.

Support is not the same thing as saving. We tend to want to save – it is a natural impulse to try to keep ourselves and the people we care about from disappointment, harm or danger. But saving puts an impossible

burden on both the saver and the saved who become caught in a cycle of rescuing and being rescued. Here there are risks of a co-dependency where the 'saver' feels caught in the never-ending impulse of helping and the 'saved' feels a disempowering burden of both expectation and indebtedness. How might a mature expression of support and caring be empowering?

Asking for support is often the bravest and wisest thing we can do for ourselves. It is an act of self-awareness. And we cannot be supportive without also being vulnerable because it is through our vulnerabilities that we can connect with and understand others. The mistake is to think that we are alone. Life is not a solo venture for most of us and asking for help reminds us where we fit into the wider pattern of life. We cannot birth ourselves. At every stage we have had to rely on help in some form or another. We can deny it or fight it but we always need our posse – our village – to support us to celebrate our joys and see our sorrows.

And equally we cannot give care and give support to others unless we also attend to our own needs, so that support can be generously given to others without expectation or the attachment of receiving in return[2] and without burnout and resentment. Also, in a cycle of reciprocity as we give to others, we also find ourselves receiving in mysterious ways.

Songlines

Practice: Asking 'What Do I Need to Ask for?'

Take a big piece of paper and your coloured pens. At the centre of the page draw yourself. And from that centre mind map all the people, places and memories which give you support and give you energy. On another piece of paper draw yourself at the centre of the page and mind map all the people, places and memories which drain your energy. Now stand back and review what you have drawn and written. Reflect on its key messages for you and think creatively about the different ways that you can further strengthen, expand and deepen your support network and ways that you can further minimize, neutralize or remove what drains you. Reflect on what you need to ask for from sources of visible and invisible help. Reflect on how your need for different types of support has changed over the years – and will change in the future – as well as how the nature of the support you give to others might also be changing. Journal your reflections.

A Journaling Practice

Ask yourself why, what, and how do I support and care? How do I allow myself to receive support or care – what are the differences here for me and what is my invitation here?

Sleep

'Sleep is the golden chain that ties our health and bodies together.'

Thomas Dekker[1]

Sleep is nature's magical panacea.

Ensuring that we get regular and good quality sleep is a precious tool in our self-care kit. It is wonderfully restorative and healing and is nature's supermedicine.

Most adults need between seven and nine hours of good quality sleep a night – so it takes up about a third of every 24-hour period. A lack of sleep – if it eludes us – can leave us frazzled and frustrated. We might feel vulnerable as we notice attention lapses, reduced cognition, delayed reactions, reduced creativity, and mood shifts. Insufficient sleep has also been linked to higher levels of risk for heart disease, diabetes, and poor mental health. But getting enough sleep is a major challenge for many of us – and the stress of it can just compound our anxieties. Our sleep can be disrupted by many different things including worry, illness and sadness.

Much has been written on the science of sleep but tuning into our own circadian rhythms (our 24-hour clock) helps us to listen to our bodies and self-regulate. Learning to match our energy levels to the task in hand helps us to find our flow and is key to our overall happiness and performance. We all know that feeling when we have to drag ourselves through the day or when we have snapped at people because we are feeling tired. Taking time out of our schedule to rest or have a short power nap or boost our energy levels through exercise can be an effective way to self-regulate. It is also a great strategy to avoid any potential disagreements stemming from the fact that we are not on top form.

There are times when we wake up in the morning with a problem that was troubling us sorted. Most people dream every night, whether or not they can remember what they dreamt about in the morning. Given its well-known health and wellbeing benefits, the question might be, why are so many of us so rest and sleep deprived? Might we need to find more energizing wholeheartedness and joy in our lives? Might exhaustion be our soul's invitation to ourselves?

Songlines

Practice: Making your Sleep your Priority

Here are some suggestions to help you maintain good 'sleep hygiene'. As you review add your own as you also decide which of these on the list needs your attention:

- Establish a realistic bedtime and keeping to it even on weekends

- Maintain a comfortable temperature in your bedroom – it might be colder than you think

- Make sure that you have a comfortable sleep environment with mattresses, pillows and bedlinen to suit your sleep preferences and body type
- Consider a screen ban for at least half an hour before going to sleep
- Avoid caffeine, alcohol and large meals just before bedtime
- Exercise during the day
- Get up if you cannot sleep after about 15 minutes and do something calming instead like making a hot drink or reading a book before trying to sleep again

A Journaling Practice

Dreams can be an interesting way into our unconscious and understanding what is going on for us deep below the surface. You can keep a Dream Journal by your bed. When you wake up in the morning, try to capture – in words or drawings – what you dreamt about. If you cannot remember – don't worry! If memories come back to you during the day just add them to your Dream Journal. Do this for a week or so and see what patterns are emerging for you. Just be curious. There is no right or wrong – and nothing to force or make happen here.

Self-Care

'Self-care is never a selfish act – it is simply good stewardship of the only gift I have, the gift I was put on earth to offer others. Anytime we can listen to true self and give the care it requires, we do it not only for ourselves, but for the many others whose lives we touch.'

Parker Palmer[1]

Good stewardship of ourselves will benefit the whole world.

Self-care is a radical and intentional practice of finding ways to consistently nourish every layer of our being, both in the present and for the future. Self-care – when practiced consistently – is a way of protecting and nurturing our own inner ecology or interiority – to resource us, to create in the moment, to put ourselves together after a setback or a loss, to boost our resilience and resourcefulness, and to help us live our dreams.

The term 'self-care' runs the risk of becoming both oversimplified and commodified as we seek quick pick-me-ups for our tiredness, skating over what we really need to sustain ourselves. Everyday surface remedies and potions – a massage, a long bath, some chocolate, a walk, or a glass of wine – all have their place, but there is more to radical self-care than that.

Homecomings

At times a pervasive anxiety or a deeper underlying exhaustion takes over – an all-encompassing fatigue, which penetrates deep inside of us and is not cured by the usual fixes of sleep, diversion or rest. This deeper exhaustion might be the result of some rupture, some removal, some disruption. It might be that a brand-new solution is required to life's events. Perhaps we are grieving for the loss of or separation from a loved one, or as a consequence of the ageing process. We tend to forget in our busy lives that about 50 per cent of life is about letting go, goodbyes and endings. It can also be our soul screaming out to us that it is feeling cramped, denied or diminished in some way. We may have moved far away from our essence. Exhaustion can be a signal that we have lost our wholehearted engagement with life – that we have neglected our own gifts and ceased to be good stewards of ourselves.

In our 'be strong and carry on' world, fatigue is seen as a weakness, but it is actually a portal into a new more tender dispensation. We can easily mistake endurance for resilience where resilience offers some scope for adaptation or shapeshifting. Endurance is the imposition of our iron will to keep going – whatever the sacrifice or personal cost. This can lead to breaking and burnout. Endurance is not resilience and it is not self-care. How then can we anticipate these tipping points before we arrive at them so that we can grow and not break? And how can we build enough regular conscious rest and stopping points to convalesce and recover?

Radical self-care is an act of tender nurturing. It is a loving commitment to our future self. In this way self-care is not an inconvenient indulgence or a designer luxury but holds the key to our own surviving, thriving and flourishing. We need self-care so we can be fully present to all the different parts of our lives and to the many roles which we are asked to occupy. It is only by putting the busyness on hold that we can become fully and truly ourselves. Self-care is also the place where our own kindness, permission, self-compassion and forgiveness meet.

Songlines

Invitation: Stocking your Pamper Self-Care Basket

Draw a picture of a basket. Ground yourself and bring to heart all the things that nourish you — for example it might be any piece of music, a book, a poem, a work of art or a film, people who inspire you, foods you love to eat, memories you cherish, jokes that makes you laugh or your little luxuries like a spa day, a favourite spot, a bubble bath or treats you fancy. Add them to your basket and remember to visit your own special basket on both good and not-so-good days to help take care of you.

A Journaling Practice

How do you nourish yourself? What is your soul-care? How can you consciously develop practices and rituals to offer you sustenance? How might these need to change over time?

Solace

'In a world of constant change and streaming technology, I find solace in the forest where a tree remains a tree.'

Angie Weiland-Crosby[1]

Solace is the home we retreat to when we need to find new and different — and perhaps more compassionate — approaches to the raw challenges and vicissitudes of life.

We can only seek the solace we need in our own way. And finding our own version of solace may be our homecoming.

To be fully human we have to risk ourselves over and over again for love. Finding consolation and solace helps us to return to love compassionately again and again, having had our hearts broken over and over. We also have to let go of much of what we previously valued or cherished. Solace gives us the grace and the equanimity to bear — but not be overwhelmed by — life itself.

Solace is comfort. It gives us the courage to remember that we have the capacity within ourselves to be with deep sorrow as well as deep love — sometimes at the same time. It also helps us dare to accept

disappointment whilst never losing hope. Solace gives us the soothing balm, easeful comfort and gentle consolations which can infuse and grace our whole being —even for a short while. Solace is the art of finding shelter and relief from the tenderness of life and living. It is not a cure or an avoidance for the faint hearted, but a strategic soothing or necessary comforting for wise living. Solace is what we must seek when we feel some sort of shape shifting or vulnerability – possibly from loss or grief, disappointment or abandonment – to help us to bear its pain. Solace is what we must also seek when we are touched by the exquisite and fragile beauty of life.

Finding our ways back to our sources of solace can be a lifetime's work. We can find our solace in a place, a person, an activity, a memory, an image, a piece of music or art, a book, a line of poetry, a turn of phrase, a moment of beauty, a glimpse of the eternal; in creativity, crafting or making or in friendships (or a combination of all of these). Here we discover how we can intentionally create the oasis we need to find equanimity and balance, and to heal.

And so, in solace we can learn how to honour our sadnesses and losses while, at the same time, finding joy, enchantment and love in our lives. We can learn how to live with heartbreak as well as wonder. We can grieve losses whilst being fully present to the bittersweet privilege and exuberance of living. We can be in the physical material realm whilst being enchanted by the magic and mystery of the ethereal and eternal.

Solace helps us to find the courage to be in the much bigger conversation of what *is*, rather than the anesthetized blanking or disassociation connected with what we feel *should* be.

We all need mementos, people and places which can offer us a place for soul work – a safe space where we can be witnessed, speak our truth, and find new compassionate ways of being.

Songlines

Practice: Finding – and Remembering – your Places of Solace

Make finding your different sources of solace your priority for a week. Collect together all the objects, mementos, photographs, quotes and lists of places and people which give you consolation, joy, enchantment and love.

Place these in a beautiful box, create a mixed media collage, add them to your journal or make a centrepiece, alter or framed picture of the all the different elements. As you connect with what you have created, feel how it greets you, sees you, hugs you, comforts you and resources you. Settle in and make yourself at home here, staying here for as long as you need, knowing you can return again and again. Here in what you have collected and curated there is nothing for you to do and nowhere else for you to go. Rest a while knowing that you are safe and held. When you have experienced its comfort, prepare to leave – perhaps bowing as you leave both to honour what your collection has given you and give thanks for the knowledge that you can always expect a warm welcome there.

A Journaling Practice

What is your relationship with solace? How, who and where do you find your solace? How do you find your balance between loss and beauty in all of its guises?

So

'Media vita in morte sumus.'
('In the midst of life we are in death.')

From Georgian Chant 'Antiphona pro Peccatis[1]

Death is a part of life.

Perhaps our ultimate homecoming is when we die – when our mortal remains return to the earth.

As Carl Jung wrote, 'Life is a luminous pause between two mysteries that are yet one[2].' Or as Nikos Kazantzakis had it, 'We come from a dark abyss, we end in a dark abyss, and we call the luminous interval life.[3]'

The cycle of creation is predicated on the cycle of birth and death, the new arising out of the space left by the passing of what was. Without death there is no life. The end is already in the beginning. It is no accident that some see death as the midwife which brings about a new stage of being.

Life with all its losses and transformations can be seen as a series of 'mini deaths' before our ultimate death. Lessons learnt from these mini deaths can help us to prepare for our own passing.

Perhaps life can only be fully lived with this acceptance of death. How might we be able to befriend and be with what many of us fear? Perhaps by reflecting on – and apprenticing ourselves to – the inevitability of our own deaths, we can find the clarity to cut through the trivia that bogs us down and focus on what truly matters.

How we choose to inhabit our own ageing bodies and our ageing processes will determine how 'youthful' we can be at any age. As we enter later life, we may move away from being defined by our multiple roles or jobs and respond to the yearnings of our soul for gentler and more profound ways of being in the world. As we move into the late summer or autumn of our lives, we start to notice that, imperceptibly, our priorities, relationships, energies and interests – as well our bodies – are subtlety changing. We start to notice that the river flow of our lives is inviting us into new dispensations, untapped possibilities and fresh directions – and probably some much-needed decluttering. These feelings may be familiar from previous life stages but – with the sense of days rapidly passing – they now feel so much more significant and urgent. We become aware that people are remembered and celebrated for what and how they loved – and not by a rollcall of their successes and achievements[4].

We sense that we are being beckoned into a new terrain which can be disorientating as it feels tinged with hints of wonder and excitement. Here – in the trajectory of our own full lives – we can feel our resistance as, paradoxically, we accept an invitation to cross over into less well known or even unknown landscapes for new or different adventures.

Crossing this threshold will bring both joy and heartache (and everything in between) as we search for new meanings, new balances, new agreements, let go to let come, and sense into a rejuvenated sense of belonging which may or may not have formal work as an element of it. This is the stepping into a new elderhood where we can value and cherish that which means the most to us. This is a time of rich spiritual development as we focus on personal learning, choice, freedom and self-expression, in the face of considerable societal pressure to conform to the cultures of ageism in our society.

So, perhaps by developing our own relationship with ageing and with death we can discover life's true nature. Our awareness of the fragility and miraculousness of it invites us to cherish every moment we have as sacred, because one of them will be our last.

Songlines

A Journaling Practice

There is the beautiful quote 'A bird does not sing because it has the answer, it sings because it has a song'[5]

And so, what is your song and what is the soundtrack to your life?

Author's Note

My original intention was that this collection would be for the fields of coaching, coaching supervision and leadership development, but encouraged by my editor I began to see this book as a collection which could reach out and speak to many people who want to find their sense of belonging in the world. The idea of 'Homecomings' originated in a café called 'Homeground' in Windermere in the Lake District, Cumbria, where we used to meet.

I know how hard it can be when we feel upset, disconnected, dislocated or uprooted. I also know that finding our ways back home to ourselves is first and foremost an inside job. And so, I wanted to create different invitational ways (with supporting practices) to help us all to explore and claim (or reclaim) the many parts of ourselves which can get lost when we stray. And to feel at home is one of the greatest privileges which a life well lived can grant us.

Acknowledgements

All books are a lifetime in the making and take a village to produce. This book is no different.

I owe a huge debt of gratitude to my loved ones who are no longer here but live on in me. To my late Mum Pearl Patterson who always made a welcoming home for me; to my late friend Lynne Richmond who always was able to tap into the beautiful and the extraordinary; and to my late supervisor Angela who always encouraged me to find my voice.

Some I am still lucky enough to journey with. To my dear sister Laura Morrissey (nee Patterson!) whose loving friendship is my bedrock; to my very patient husband Steve whose good-humoured support of me and my creativity is enduring and gives me the encouragement to keep going; to our very spirited adopted daughter Naomi whose search for the meaning of home always keeps me inspired and humbled; to my great friend Caroline Lambert whose friendship and support is priceless; and to our dog Lara who always makes me laugh! Also, my dear friend Karyn Prentice who is my fellow writer, soul sister and creative partner. Together we are PattersonPrenticeDesigns. Karyn's presence in my life is just magical. I forever bless the day we met and the work of radical hope that we co-create to take out into the world.

Homecomings

I also want to thank my wonderful editor Emma Dickens whose loving care and wisdom sits within every edited line of this book. Thanks also Alessandra from 'Send Love from Paris' on Etsy who designed the beautiful vintage stamps and to Andy Meaden of Meaden Creative whose imaginative designs have helped us to bring this book alive.

And finally, I want to thank everyone I have ever met and worked with – as well as to the many writers of the many articles and books I have read. Your wisdom has touched me and your insights and spirit sit within these lines.

End Notes

Route Mapping

Stilling

[1] Downloaded 20th June 2022 from www.goodreads.com

[2] *Ibid.*

[3] Downloaded 27th May 2021 from https://www.mindful.org/everyday-mindfulness-with-jon-kabat-zinn/

[4] This is a reference to the famous lines written by T. S. Elliot in The Four Quartets:

> At the still point of the turning world. Neither flesh nor fleshless;
> Neither from nor towards; at the still point, there the dance is,
> But neither arrest nor movement. And do not call it fixity,
> Where past and future are gathered. Neither movement from nor towards,
> Neither ascent nor decline. Except for the point, the still point,
> There would be no dance, and there is only the dance.

[5] As cited in *Lao Tzu, Tao Te Ching,* Chapter 15

Sanctuary

[1] Hersey, T. (2015) *Sanctuary – Creating a Space for Grace in your Life*. Chicago, Loyola Press

[2] Joseph Campbell cited in Woodbury, D. (2013) *5 Tips for Creating a Sacred Space*. Downloaded on 19th September 2017 from http://www.huffingtonpost.com/debbie-woodbury/sacred-space_b_3094267.html

[3] From https://www.tate.org.uk/art/artworks/blake-the-fall-of-satan-a00027

Slow

[1] Downloaded on 7th June 2022 from www.brainyquote.com

[2] Notes: 'The Slow Movement' is a subculture which is centred on slowing down life's pace. In Carl Honore's 2004 book *In Praise of Slow* he described the Slow Movement as 'a cultural revolution against the notion that faster is always better. The Slow philosophy is not about doing everything at a snail's pace. It is about seeking to do everything at the right speed. Savouring the hours and the minutes rather than just counting them. Doing everything as well as possible, instead as fast as possible. It is about quality rather than quantity.' It started with Carlo Petrini's protest against the opening of a McDonalds in Rome in the 1980s which sparked 'slow food' and has now extended into many other areas like 'slow transport', 'slow cities', 'slow books', 'slow schools', 'slow money' and 'slow living'. It is also associated with sustainability, localism, and improving the quality of life by celebrating culture and social connection

Silence

[1] Downloaded 4th September 2017 from http://thinkexist.com/quotation/see_how_nature-trees-flowers-grass-grows_in/149761.html

Solitude

[1] Downloaded 5th September 2017 from https://www.brainpickings.org/2014/12/17/wendell-berry-pride-despair-solitude/

Start

[1] Downloaded 8th March 2022 from www.movementquotes.com/top-10-take-action-quotes.

Safety

[1] Downloaded on 5th July 2022 from www.brainyquote.com

[2] See the work of Bowlby, J. (1969) *Attachment and Loss:* Volume 1. Attachment, New York, Basic Books

Senses

[1] Downloaded 12th May 2021 from www.fancyquote.com

[2] Scharmer, O.C. (2018) *The Essentials of Theory U – Core Principles and Applications.* Pp 9. California, Berrett-Koehler Publications

[3] See Van Der Kolb's work on *The Body Keeps the Score – Mind, Brain and Body in the Transformation of Trauma* published by Penguin

Soul

[1] O'Donohue (1997) *Anam Cara: Spiritual Wisdom From the Celtic World.* London, Bantam Books

[2] Notes: the words 'soul' and 'spirit' are often used interchangeably and are confusing. This is my interpretation – but please differentiate (or not) in ways that work for you. The *Oxford English Dictionary* defines 'soul' as 'the spiritual or immaterial part of us which is held to survive our deaths'. 'Spirit' is defined as 'The animating or vital principle held to give life to physical organisms or the non-physical part of a person which is the seat of their soul – their emotions and character.'

Self

[1] With thanks to the daily quote feed from the Network for Grateful Living 17th April 2021

[2] The concept of the little 'self' and bigger 'Self' is taken from the field of Transpersonal Psychology. The smaller 'self' is ego and the bigger 'Self' is the smaller 'self' awakened

[3] Kumar, S. (2002) *You Are Because I Am: A Declaration of Dependence*. UK, Green Books

[4] Adapted from 'The Chronicles of Narnia' by C. S. Lewis

Soul Friends

[1] O'Donohue, J. (1997) *Anam Cara: Spiritual Wisdom from the Celtic World*. Pg 41. London, Bantam Books

[2] In his *Ethics*, Aristotle grounds friendship on the ideas of goodness and beauty – and defines a friend as someone who wishes what is good for the other. In the Buddhist tradition, the anam cara is called a 'kalyana-mitra' or 'noble friend'

States of Being

[1] Downloaded on 10th February 2023 from www.bookroocom

Sacred

[1] Downloaded 9th March 2023 from A–Z Quotes

Salute

[1] Downloaded 10th November 2021 from AZ Quotes

[2] Rainer Maria Rilke (1946) *Selected Letters*. Trans. R. F. C. Hull. London, Macmillan & Co.

Footprints

Seasons

[1] Downloaded 5th May 2021 from https://www.brainyquote.com/quotes/frank_lloyd_wright_127707

[2] Prentice, K. (2020) *Nature's Way: Designing the Life you Want Through the Lens of Nature and the Five Seasons*. UK, Milton Keynes

[3] For more information see www.wearejapan.com. Leaning heavily on the Chinese almanac, Japan's poetic year starts with risshun, the 'birth of spring' in early February and ends with daikan, or 'greater cold' in late January. With a level of precision far beyond anything we in the West can imagine, the sub-seasons between are then divided into three micro-seasons, observing subtle shifts in the natural world with evocative names such as 'fish emerge from the ice', 'wild geese return' and 'mist starts to linger'. Encouraging a close observation of the passing months, each ko lasts approximately five days, serving as a poetic, mindful journey through Japan's ever-changing landscape

Homecomings

Savour

[1] Downloaded 16th September 2021 from https://www.brainyquote.com/quotes/diane_ackerman_104441

[2] Reference *Oxford English Dictionary*

'Seeing' Another

[1] Downloaded 12th April 2021 from https://www.goodreads.com/quotes/tag/i-see-you

[2] There are multiple sources of quality for this story, including for example Wells, L. (2003). The Net of Indra. In Cox, A. & Albert, D. (eds.), *The Healing Heart: Communities Storytelling to Build Strong and Healthy Communities* (p. 50). Gabriola Island, BC: New Society Publishers

[3] 'No man is an island' is a famous line from 'Devotions Upon Emergent Occasions', a 1624 prose work by the English poet John Donne

Soften

[1] Downloaded om 13th March 2023 from www.grateful.org

Sadness

[1] E. A. Bucchianeri from 'Brushstrokes of a Gadfly'. Downloaded from www.goodreads.com/sadness

[2] Sadness is one of the six basic emotions described by Paul Ekman. The others are happiness, anger, surprise, fear and disgust

[3] Richter, Jean Paul F. (1842) *Selina*. Gale ECCO, Print Editions Online

Surrender

[1] Downloaded 11th May 2017 from https://www.goodreads.com/

quotes/538827-beyond-our-ideas-of-right-doing-and-wrong-doing-there-is-a

[2] Sisyphus, a figure of Greek mythology who was condemned to repeat forever the same meaningless task of pushing a boulder up a mountain, only to see it roll down again

[3] In Engineering, the yield point is the point on a stress-strain curve that indicates the limit of elastic behaviour and the beginning plastic behaviour

[4] The phoenix is a long-lived bird associated with Greek mythology that cyclically regenerates or is otherwise born again. Associated with the sun, a phoenix obtains new life by arising from the ashes of its predecessor

Shadow

[1] This is the tagline Thich Nhat Nanh's book *The Art of Transforming Suffering*

[2] Inspired by a paper called 'The Shadowlands of Winter' from PattersonPrenticeDesign's paper for the EMCC Global EQA Practitioner Diploma 'Cultivating and Choreographing the Rich Tapestry of Wholehearted Creativity'

Suffering

[1] Downloaded on 22nd November 2021 from www.goodreads.com

[2] Please see Practice Inquiry 13 – 'The Buddhist Arrow of Pain and Pleasure' in *Reflect to Create!*

[3] From Leonard Cohen's song 'Anthem' Live in London on YouTube www.watch?v=c8–BT66_wYg

[4] Dalai Lama (2011) *A Profound Mind – Cultivating Wisdom in Everyday Life.* Pp 43. London, Hodder and Stoughton

[5] Downloaded 2nd October 2023 from www.goodreads.com

Stagnation

[1] Downloaded on 9th November 2021 from www.goodreads.com

[2] Cameron, J. (1998) *The Right to Write.* Pp 77. New York, Hay House Publishing

Shape

[1] The poem 'Working Together' was written by David Whyte for the presentation of the Collier Trophy to the Boeing Company marking the introduction of the new 777 passenger jet

[2] Inspired by Bessel Van der Kolb's book *The Body Keeps the Score: Mind, Brain and Body in the Transformation of Trauma* published in 2015 by Penguin

Stories

[1] Brown, J. (2012) Poem 'The Stories We Tell Ourselves' was cited in *The Art and Spirit of Leadership.* Pp 302. USA, Trafford Publishing

[2] For more information please see Berne, E. (2016) *Games People Play: The Psychology of Human Relationships.* London, Penguin Life

Shame

[1] Brown, B. (2010) *The Gifts of Imperfection – Let Go of Who You Think You are Supposed to Be and Embrace Who You Are. Your Guide to Wholehearted Living.* Minnesota, Hazeldene

Sublime

[1] Downloaded 31stJanuary 2022 from www.goodreads.com

[2] From James Hillman Eranos Lecture 2 Spring 1981 Publications *"Thoughts of the Heart"*. Downloaded 31st January 2022 from www.compilerpress.ca

[3] The **Beauty Way** is derived from **Hózhó**, the Navajo word for the concept of living in a holistic environment of Beauty, Balance, Harmony, and Well-Being.

Seeking

[1] Whyte, D. (2007) *River Flow – New and Selected Poems 1984 to 2007*. Langley, Many Rivers Press. Pp 348

[2] After James Hillman and his book *The Souls Code – In Search of Character and Calling* published in 1997 by Bantam

[3] This is taken from *Dubliners*, a collection of 15 short stories by James Joyce, first published in 1914. The stories depict Irish middle class life and centre on Joyce's idea of an epiphany: a moment where a character experiences self-understanding or illumination. In 'A Painful Case', Joyce writes, 'Mr. Duffy lived a short distance from his body' and goes on to explore the meaning of this disconnection

[4] Downloaded on 5th December 2022 from www.goodreads.com

Serendipity

[1] Downloaded on 17th January 2020 from www.vbchnage.com

[2] For more information on the history of magic please see www.britannica.com/topic/magic/-supernatural-phenomenon/History-of-magic-in-Western-Worldviews

Homecomings

Scanning

[1] Downloaded 12th April 2023 from www.azquotes.com

Symbols and Sideways Thinking

[1] Downloaded 13th December 2021 from www.brainyquote.com

[2] Carl Jung believed that there exists a pre-experiential set of mythological motifs, archetypes or combination of images and ideas which can be found in the myths of our own communities and which yield a shared collective consciousness

[3] The idea of 'overfishing' is borrowed from *The Right to Write: An Invitation and Initiation into the Writing Life* by Julia Cameron published by Hay House in the UK

Surprise

[1] Downloaded 31st August 2021 from www. brainyquote.com

[2] Adapted from a paper for the PattersonPrenticeDesign's year long programme "Cultivating and Choreographing the Rich Tapestry of Wholehearted Creativity which was posted in LinkedIn in May 2021

[3] The poem 'A Bride Married to Amazement' was published by Mary Oliver in her book *Devotions – The Selected Poems by Mary Oliver*, in 2017 by Penguin Press

Simplicity

[1] Downloaded 27th May 2021 from www.goodreads.com

[2] The term 'eye of a needle' is used as a metaphor for a very narrow opening. It occurs several times throughout the *Talmud*. The New Testament quotes Jesus as saying 'it is easier for a camel to go through

the eye of a needle than for a rich man to enter the kingdom of God' Matthew 19:24

[3] These are known as the 'Kanchukas' and are Dharana 72 in 'The Vigyana Bhairava' – a text which some say formed the basis of Zen Buddhism. The Kanchukas are seen as coverings or limitations which take us out of present moment awareness

Silliness

[1] Downloaded on 16th February 2022 from www.goodreads.com

[2] For more information on Transactional Analysis please see Berne, E. (1964) *The Games People Play – The Psychology of Human Relationships*. USA, Grove Press, Inc.

Souvenir

[1] Downloaded on 8th March 2022 from www.goodreads.com

[2] The nine muses from Greek mythology which were considered the source of knowledge are Calliope for epic poetry, Clio for history, Euterpe for flutes and music, Thalia for comedy and pastoral poetry, Melpomene for tragedy, Terpsichore for dance, Eroto for love, poetry and lyrical poetry, Polyhymnia for hymns and sacred poetry and Urania for astronomy

[3] *Oxford English Dictionary* (1976) Pp 947

Rest and Return

Strolling

[1] Downloaded 15th February 2022 from www.goodreads.com

Homecomings

Spirit as Love

[1]   Downloaded 16th June 2017 from http://azquotes.com

[2]   Downloaded on 12th May 2021 from https://tracyseed.com/love-energy/

'The Universal Force of Love' – A letter thought to be written by Albert Einstein to his daughter, Liesel

[3]   Downloaded 1st November 2017 from http://thinkexist.com/quotation/your_task_is_not_to_seek_love

Skills for Life

[1]   Downloaded on 16th December from www.goodreads.com

[2]   See Chapter 4 'The Prelude' in *Reflect to Create! The Dance of Reflection for Creative Leadership, Professional Practice and Supervision*. London, Centre of Reflection and Creativity Ltd.

[3]   From (2010) 'The Way of Chuang Tzu' by Thomas Merton. New York, New Direction

Study

[1]   Downloaded 15th March 2021 from https://www.goodreads.com/quotes/tag/study

[2]   Here I took inspiration from the work of Benjamin and Rosaland Zander and their book *The Art of Possibility*. I love the concept of the A* student, so very different from my own memories of my school days

[3]   I was inspired here by Rumi's evergreen poetry:

> Out beyond ideas of wrongdoing and right doing there is a field. I'll meet you there.

> When the soul lies down in that grass
> the world is too full to talk about.

Stitching

[1] Downloaded on 13th March 2023 from www.quiltdom.com

[2] The Practice Finding your Golden Thread is inspired by my work with Karyn Prentice in our programme "Cultivating and Choreographing the Rich Tapestry of your Wholehearted Creativity.

Structure

[1] Downloaded 3rd October 2023 from www.goodreads.com from 'The Story of Philosophy'

Strength as Courage

[1] Downloaded 9th March 2023 from www.goodreads.com

[2] Pali is a Middle Indo-Aryan liturgical language native to the Indian subcontinent

Service

[1] Downloaded 16th January 2018 from https://www.goodreads.com

Society

[1] In a Vimeo video by Planetary Collective called 'Overview', David Beaver, co-founder of the Overview Institute, recounts the sentiments from one of the astronauts on the Apollo mission: 'When we originally went to the Moon, our total focus was on the Moon. We weren't thinking about looking back at the Earth. But now that we've done it, that may well have been the most important reason we went.'

[2] Zen Master Thich Nhat Hanh was a global spiritual leader, poet, author, and peace activist, revered around the world for his pioneering teachings and writings on mindfulness, global ethics, and peace

Stewardship

[1] Downloaded 11th July 2023 from www.goodreads.com

Sharing

[1] Downloaded 10th February 2023 from 222.goodreads.com.

[2] See Kimmerer, R.W. (2020) *Braiding Sweetgrass: Indigenous Wisdom, Scientific Knowledge and the Teachings of Plants.* New York, Penguin

Sorry

[1] Downloaded 29th November 2021 from www.keepinspiringme.com

Support

[1] Downloaded 11th October 2021 from www.goodreads.com

Sleep

[1] Downloaded 13th March 2023 from www.senseacalm.com

Self-care

[1] Palmer. P.J (2000) *Let your Life Speak – Listening to the Voice of Vocation.* San Francisco, Jossey-Bass

Solace

[1] Downloaded 13th January 2022 from www.angieweilandcrosby.com

So

[1] Downloaded on 2nd August 2023 from Wikipedia.org

[2] Downloaded 3rd October 2023 from www.DiscoverQuotes.com, 2021. October 2023. https://discoverquotes.com/carl-jung/quote1481196/

[3] ***Ascesis: The Saviors of God*** is a series of spiritual exercises written by Greek Author Nikos Kazantazakis It was first written between 1922 and 1923, while staying in Vienna and Berlin, and subsequently published in 1927 in the Athenian magazine Anayennisi

[4] Inspired from the brochure that Karyn Prentice and I have designed for our programme 'Bridging the Unknown: From Role Work to Soul Calling in Later Life.

[5] Downloaded 18th October from www.quotesgram.com

Bibliography and Reading List

Abram, D. (1997/2017) *The Spell of the Sensuous*. US Vintage Books

Artess, L. (2006) *The Sacred Path Companion – A Guide to Walking the Labyrinth to Heal and Transform*. New York, Riverhead Books

Barks, C. (trans) (2007) *Rumi Bridge to the Soul, Journeys into the Music and Silence of the Heart*. New York, HarperCollins

Beer, A. (2020) *Every Day Nature – How Noticing Nature Can Quietly Change your Life*. London, National Trust.

Brown, B. (2010) *The Gifts of Imperfection: Let Go of Who You Think You're Supposed to Be and Embrace Who You Are. Your Guide to Wholehearted Living*. Minnesota, Hazelden

Brown, B. (2012) *Daring Greatly How the Courage to Be Vulnerable Transforms the Way We Live, Love, Parent and Lead*. London, Penguin Group

Cameron, J. (1996) *The Vein of Gold – A Journey to Your Creative Heart*. USA, Tarcher/Putman

Cameron, J. (2016) *It's Never Too Late to Begin Again – Discovering Creativity and Meaning at Midlife and Beyond.* New York, Tarcherperigree

Campbell, J. (2012) *The Hero with a Thousand Faces. 3rd Edition.* San Francisco, New World Library

Chodron, P. (2001) *Start Where You Are: A Guide to Compassionate Living.* USA, Shambhala Publications

Crumley, J. (2017) *The Nature of the Seasons Series.* UK, Saraband

Foster, J. (2013) *Falling in Love with Where You Are: A Year of Prose and Poetry on Radically Opening Up to the Pain and Joy of Life.* Salisbury, Non Duality Press

Fox, M. (2002) *Creativity – Where the Divine and Human Meet.* New York, Tarcher/Putman Books

Frankl, V. (1959) *Man's Search for Meaning – The Classic Tribute to Hope in the Holocaust.* London, Rider

Fredrickson, B (2014), *Love 2:0.* New York, Penguin

Gilbert, E. (2015) *Big Magic – Creative Living Beyond Fear.* London, Bloomsbury Publishing

Gilligan, S. And Dilts, R. (2009) *The Hero's Journey: A Voyage of Self Discovery.* Carmarthen, Crown House Publishing Ltd.

Harris, M. (2017) *Solitude – In Pursuit of a Singular Life in a Crowded World.* London, Random House Books

Harrison, M. (Editor) (2016) *Seasons (A4 Volume Anthology)* UK, The Wild Life Trust

Hershey, T, (2000) Soul Gardening, *Cultivating the Good Life,* Minneapolis, Augsburg Fortress

Hooks, B. (2009) *Belonging – A Culture of Place.* New York, Routledge

Hollis, J. (1993) *The Middle Passage: From Misery to Meaning in Mid-Life (Studies in Jungian Psychology by Jungian Analysts).* London, Inner City Books

Hollis, J. (2000) *Creating a Life: Finding your Individual Path.* London, Inner City Books

Humble, K. 92023) *Where the Hearth Is – Stories of Home.* UK, Octopus Publishing Group

Kagge, E. (2017) *Silence in the Age of Noise.* London, Viking

Kimmerer, R. W. (2013) *Braiding Sweetgrass – Ingenious Wisdom, Scientific Knowledge and the Teachings of Plants.* UK, Penguin Random House UK

Khan, S (2021) *What is Home, Mum?* Oxford, New Internationalist Publications

Kornfield, J. (1993) *A Path with Heart.* New York, Bantam Books

Kornfield, J. (2008) *The Wise Heart – Buddhist Psychology for the West.* USA, Rider

Markova, D. (2021) *I Will Not Live an Unlived Life – Reclaiming Passion and Purpose.* Florida, Conari Press

Moore, T. (1992) *Care of the Soul: An Inspirational Programme to Add Depth and Meaning to Your Everyday Life.* UK, Piatkus Books

Neff, K. (2011) *Self-Compassion Stop Beating Yourself Up and Leave Insecurity Behind.* Hodder and Stoughton Ltd, London

Nepo, M. (2014) *The Endless Practice – Becoming Who You Were Born to Be.* New York, Atria Paperback

O'Donohue, J. (1998) *Anam Cara: A Book of Celtic Wisdom.* New York, Harper Perennial

O'Donohue, J. (2008) *To Bless the Space Between Us: A Book of Blessings.* USA, Sounds True Inc.

O'Donohue, J, (2015) *Walking in Wonder Eternal Wisdom for a Modern World,* New York, Crown Publishers

Oliver, M. (2017) *Devotions: The Selected Poems of Mary Oliver.* London, Penguin Press

Oliver, M. (2019) *A Thousand Mornings.* USA, Corsair Publishing

Oriah Mountain Dreamer (2001) *The Dance – Moving to the Deep Rhythms of Your Life.* USA, HarperCollins Publishers

Paintner, C.V. (2011) *The Artist's Rule – A Twelve Week Journey Nurturing your Creative Soul with Monastic Wisdom.* USA, Sorin Books.

Palmer, P. J. (2000) *Let Your Life Speak – Listening for the Voice of Vocation.* San Francisco, Jossey-Bass

Palmer, P. J. (2007) *The Courage to Teach: Guide for Reflection and Renewal.* San Francisco, Jossey-Bass

Palmer, P.J. (1990) *The Active Life – A Spirituality of Work, Creativity and Caring.* San Francisco, Jossey-Bass

Palmer, P.J. (2004) *A Hidden Wholeness – The Journey Toward an Undivided Life Welcoming Soul and Weaving Community in a Wounded World.* San Francisco, John Wiley and Sons, Inc.

Patterson, E. (2019) *Reflect to Create! The Dance of Reflection for Creative Leadership, Professional Practice and Supervision.* London, Centre for Reflection and Creativity Ltd.

Prentice, K. (2019) *Nature's Way: Designing the Life you Want through the Lens of Nature and the Five Seasons.* Milton Keynes, Prentice Fletcher Associates

Reman, R. N. (2006) *Kitchen Table Wisdom: Stories that Heal.* Hull, Riverhead Books

Reman, R. N. (2001) *My Grandfather's Blessings: Stories of Strength, Refuge and Belonging.* UK, G.P. Putman and Sons

Salzburg, S (2002) *Loving Kindness – The Revolutionary Art of Happiness*, Massachusetts, Shambhala Publications

Salzberg, S. (2015) *The Kindness Handbook: A Practical Companion.* Colorado, Sounds True

Scharmer, O. (2018) *The Essentials of Theory U – Core Principles and Applications.* California, Berrett-Koehler Publishers Inc.

Solnit, R. (2017) *A Field Guide to Getting Lost.* New York, Viking Book

Sunim, Haemin and Kim, Chi-Young, (2018) *The Things You Can See Only When You Slow Down.* London, Penguin

Tolle, E. (1999) *The Power of Now – A Guide to Spiritual Enlightenment.* USA, New World Library

Whyte, D. (2007) *Many Rivers Flow.* Langley, Many Rivers Press

Whyte, D. (2015) *Consolations: The Solace, Nourishment and Underlying Meaning of Everyday Words.* Langley, Many Rivers Press

Zweig, C. (2021) *The Inner Work of Age: Shifting from Role to Soul.* Vermont, Park Street Press

The Guest House

This being human is a guest house.
Every morning a new arrival.

A joy, a depression, a meanness,
some momentary awareness comes
as an unexpected visitor.

Welcome and entertain them all!
Even if they're a crowd of sorrows,
who violently sweep your house
empty of its furniture,
still, treat each guest honourably.
He may be clearing you out
for some new delight.

The dark thought, the shame, the malice,
meet them at the door laughing,
and invite them in.

Be grateful for whoever comes,
because each has been sent
as a guide from beyond.

Rumi (trans. Coleman Barks)

Milton Keynes UK
Ingram Content Group UK Ltd.
UKHW020957181024
449752UK00008B/93